AMERICA
at the TIPPING POINT

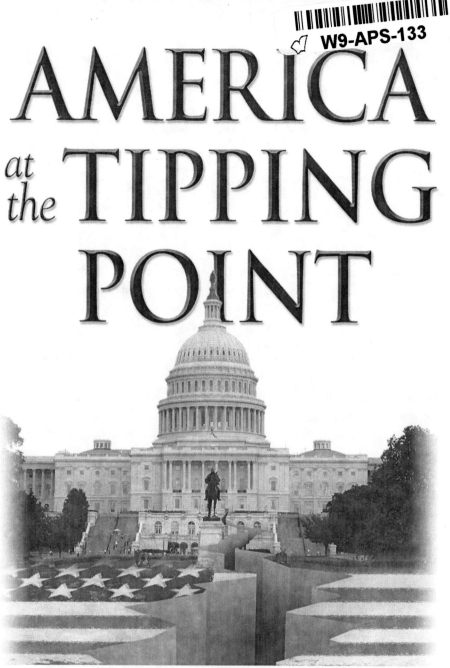

GARY FRAZIER

with Jennifer Rast and Helen Hosier

**Author's
PUBLISHER**
The New Generation of Publishing

AMERICA
at the
TIPPING POINT

© 2009 Gary Frazier

ISBN: 978-0-9817009-2-2 Paperback

Published by:

Author's Publisher
14805 Forest Road, Suite 106
Forest, VA 24551
www.AuthorsPublisher.com

This Book Is Dedicated To:

The faithful followers of the Lord Jesus Christ,

Every American who has and is standing
for what is right,

My children and grandchildren who are in peril
because of decisions being made that will affect
their lives long after I am gone.

ACKNOWLEDGEMENTS

I would like to thank Jennifer Rast and Helen Hosier for their tireless efforts in helping research this book. Jennifer worked countless hours researching topics and sharing her thoughts often at the expense of her own health. In addition Helen gave her usual "all for the Kingdom" tirelessly helping bring all my thoughts together.

In addition, I dare not fail to mention retired Congressman William E. Dannemeyer of California whose incredible insights in the 1980's stirred my mind and soul. His insightful book, *A Shadow in the Land: Homosexuality in America* seems today to be a prophetic word from the past. While I may not agree with the Congressman on every issue, his courage challenges me and I thank God for his service to America.

CONTENTS

INTRODUCTION

This book is something of a departure for me. In my past books I have written about the indicators present in our world that point out we are living in the end times and that Christ Jesus is coming again very, very soon. However, as a history buff and one who watches trends and events, I see what has happened in America and the path it appears we have chosen and I find myself greatly alarmed. Were it not for my faith, hope and trust in the sovereignty of God and my understanding of His mercy and compassion, and that He is ultimately in control, I would be frightened. For this reason I feel compelled to address this for I see America at a tipping point and the Word of God commands as Christians we are to stand in the gap and sound the warning.

Allow me to put you, the reader, on notice. This is not a feel good, warm fuzzy message. Rather it is the sounding of the alarm calling all Americans to the battle to save this great country as we slip ever so quickly toward the abyss. The apathy, indifference, disregard, misinformation…the list could get long…of what has taken place in recent years gives cause for concern. The idea of individual freedom, very little government interference, and the quest for prosperity; the dreams and aspirations to be free from tyranny that brought this country into existence, seemingly are being tossed aside like rubbage. Is it because our schools have slowly been transformed into institutions of cultural change instead of halls of learning how to read, write, work math problems, study history and geography and seek to learn, understand and apply the principles of citizenship? Is the emphasis no longer on these facts? What do students know about the sacrifices and dreams of our Founding Fathers, the Presidents who have led this great nation, the many times Americans have fought and died for the very freedoms we take for granted today? How much of this great American story do they truly know and comprehend? America is at a Tipping Point in the classroom! A look at this is included in this book.

Additionally, I will share my grave concern with regard to the all-out war on the faith and values held dear by millions of followers of our Lord Jesus Christ. Never has there been so much rhetoric by so many about tolerance with so little being exhibited. The Constitution of this great country provides for the freedom OF religion, not freedom FROM religion. America is at a Tipping Point with regard to our freedom to worship as believers in and followers of Christ and the battle rages daily in the courts across this land. Can any nation survive who attempts to live in a sterile environment excluding the God who created the world and all that is within?

Civilized nations have always treasured and protected life understanding the value of this most basic and precious gift. Pagan nations around the globe have sacrificed their children upon the altar to their pagan deities, yet since 1973 more than 40 million of our most precious have been murdered. How can this take place we ask? The answer is quite simple really, change the way people look at conception and dehumanize the child! I am driven to keep this debate alive in our hearts and minds.

As an American in his sixties I never dreamed I would turn on the tube and see homosexuals, lesbians and other perversions marching in our streets demanding so-called equal rights! Yet today we are being force fed a steady diet of these various forms of perversion, all the while being told we must accept this as normal. God forbid!

As I write these words America is embroiled in a controversy over euthanasia and the right to die. Thinking people have long known the logical conclusion of abortion is euthanasia. The words we are hearing daily are "quality of life" and, as the economy in America tanks, there are those who are telling us hard choices will have to be made since health care costs are so high and funds so limited. Is America prepared for this kind of choosing who will live and who will die? We have seen this before in a place called Nazi Germany.

Greed, loss of civility, a self perpetuating governmental bureaucracy and a Supreme Court where a small group of elitists rule over the masses, is a huge shift away from what our founders had in mind when they laid it all on the line by signing the Declaration of Independence and later the Constitution. These are issues I am compelled to address.

By the time this book is published many changes will have already taken place in our nation and many others will be under consideration. The mainstream media has made a decision to stop reporting the news and produce it instead; all the while making sure the average American is kept in the dark without any real answers to the tough questions of our day. In fact, and I don't like saying this, but the world view of the majority of Americans is what can you do for me? It is a self-centered, take-all-attitude that looks to the government to supply their needs. People will give up all their rights to be "taken care of." Is this what the American people really want?

It is time we stand up and speak out. America is at a Tipping Point that could spell our demise! If we do not get involved, if we do not sound the alarm we may lose this great land. If not me, if not you, then who, if not now, when?

CHAPTER ONE

A COUNTRY MEANT FOR GREATNESS

We shall nobly save or meanly lose this last best hope of earth.

President Abraham Lincoln

(A letter to Congress in December 1862, shortly after he issued the preliminary Emancipation Proclamation.)

During an evening performance of "The Tonight Show," Comedian Jay Leno asked the audience if anyone could name just one of the Ten Commandments — a task most children who have attended Sunday school even briefly should be able to do. A member of the audience proudly, but incorrectly, responded, "God helps those who help themselves." So typical of our society today, this individual not only had no idea what the Ten Commandments were, the only religious sounding phrase they could quote from memory was about as far from any kind of commandment as you can get, and isn't found in the Bible. It makes sense that our self-absorbed society would lead this person to recall *what God can do for them* in response to a question asking *what God requires of us.*

As research performed at Wheaton College several years ago has demonstrated, this complete ignorance of even the most basic biblical concepts is all too common in today's society. Even among those who claim to be Bible-believing Christians, there is a lamentable lack of biblical knowledge, leading to a muddled, secularized version of the Gospel being spread by those who should know the Bible the best. False views of Christianity are compounded by distortions of Scripture, like the one above, commonly cited by secularists, usually in an attempt to support their humanist world view. For instance, one of the secularists' favorite snippets of Scripture is "judge not, lest ye be judged." Taking this completely out of context, they argue that Christians must accept everything, whether it agrees with the Bible or not, and abandon any judgment of the world around them, lest their own God be angry with them. Ironically, they don't recognize their criticism of Christian beliefs and opinions as passing judgment on another human being's beliefs and actions.

Only a humanist could use Scripture to pass judgment while rebuking a believer for using their knowledge of Scripture to make evaluations. If you can get them to recognize their circular logic, nine times out of ten they'll try to sum up the entire Bible in Jesus' command to "love one another." To them, being loved is getting your way, never being challenged, never being disagreed with, corrected, or punished. Yet, if they'd actually read the Bible they would know that, while God loves us as His children, He also has rules, criticisms, and punishment when those rules aren't followed. As with any good parent, God in His love makes demands based on what He knows is good for us. In the same way, Christians who bring attention to the wickedness of this country, and the moral decline of what was once a Christian nation, are doing the most loving thing they could. While society might think we're being judgmental and intolerant, doing anything less would be to tolerate them right into hell. God will be the final judge, but you might say Christians are to be the early warning system for those who are perishing.

There was a time in America when Christianity was such a force among the population, no one would have conceived that there would be a time when the mere mention of the Bible, or anything in it, could be seen as being judgmental and intolerant. Christianity wasn't just the Gospel of the "religious right," it was the foundation for the government, the schools, the legal system, and the lives of the vast majority of those who chose to immigrate to the New World. God's standard, His eternal wisdom, applies to everyone and the Founding Fathers recognized this.

To listen to the political Left today who claim to be the most "tolerant," is to see without much, if any, effort that they are the most intolerant of all. It could rightly be called the intolerance of tolerance. Demonizing labels are cast upon those who hold differing views; what is said is called "hate speech." There is no such thing as an absolute right and wrong, we are to accept all viewpoints as being equally valid. That is nothing but a recipe for social chaos, an America at the tipping point which we see today.

OUR FOUNDERS READ IT AND BELIEVED IT

When this country was just being born, George Washington kissed the Bible at his inaugural ceremonies. The sovereignty of the God of the Bible was mentioned in the Mayflower Compact, the Declaration of Independence, and the Constitution; it is written on our currency and in our oaths, and God is mentioned in all fifty state constitutions, as well as in the Pledge of Allegiance. What has happened to the God-fearing country that was founded by faithful followers of Christ? Our Founding Fathers saw the Bible and the Scriptures within as the source of the guiding principles that should be the foundation for our constitution, laws, democratic system of government, and the nation's judicial system. Our seventh President, Andrew Jackson, said concerning the Bible, *"That book, sir, is the Rock upon which our Republic rests."* Not only was that the opinion of President Jackson, but also the sentiment of countless Americans.

If only all citizens would hear, know, and remember these thought-provoking sentiments. For those of us who *do* know, how good it is to reflect, for instance, on what President Abraham Lincoln, our sixteenth president, said: *"In regard to this Great Book, I have this to say, it is the best gift God has given to men. All the Good Savior gave to the world was communicated through this book."*

It seems sadly, that so many Americans today have kissed the Bible goodbye. Americans have been slowly, but surely, handing over the freedoms that were given to us by God to an increasingly powerful government. If it gets God out of their lives, they are willing to give up rights that Americans once viewed as being worth fighting for. To America's founders, a people who had experienced the despotism and lack of freedom under the monarchies and dictators of Europe, life under God's rule and God's rule alone was the only true freedom.

WHERE DO OUR FREEDOMS AND RIGHTS COME FROM?

This attitude toward God is seen most clearly in our schools where we are teaching our children to willingly forfeit their God-given rights in exchange for the discriminatory will of politicians, government lawyers, and activist judges. It also must be acknowledged that the politics of their parents, and one could also say, parental neglect, are making future generations incapable of recognizing the erosion of personal freedoms and the rights that our ancestors once fought and died to protect. To the concern of many, our nation is now drifting from its biblical foundations.

In this chapter, we will explore the foundations that made this country great, and the men and women who began anew in this New World with the hope of providing for their children a Christian nation where they could worship freely. It is this foundation that is our only hope, if we have the will to fight back against those who have led us down a road of moral depravity to a repeat of Sodom and Gomorrah. President Abraham Lincoln rightly called it *"our last best hope."* Men and women have fought, and are fighting, to preserve that hope. What a price they have and are paying! How awful if we today let it slip away through indifference and a blatant disregard for what is right and just.

WHAT HAPPENED TO GOD?

The story of America's decline begins in the pages of our history books — books that are seldom opened in our classrooms today, or have been rewritten for the purposes of indoctrinating our children with a completely revisionist version of our nation's heritage and history. In addition to studying the true history and Christian heritage of America, we will explore in this book the judicial activism and moral relativism that began the process of kicking God out of our government, our schools, and our lives. To truly understand what has been lost over the short 230-plus-year history of this great country, we must first understand where we began.

REWRITING HISTORY FOR A CHANGING CULTURE

America was founded by Christians, who saw the teachings of Jesus Christ as the foundation upon which the nation's governing bodies were to be built, and it was once accepted as historical fact. Today, however, it's not uncommon to hear this historical fact disputed and dismissed, even among highly educated people and university professors. So successful have been the purveyors of revisionist history, that many Americans now graduating from our institutions of higher learning have no idea that America was once an undeniably Christian nation.

We are surrounded by the evidence of this history in our government buildings, artwork, monuments, and in most of the documents written by America's Founding Fathers. Yet, these evidences have been omitted from our nation's textbooks under the guise of "separation of Church and State." We are left with a version of history that our founders would not have recognized, nor would they have wanted to be a part of. I can envision them standing up and shouting, *"NO! NO! NO! This is not what was meant!"*

Let me impress upon your thinking to such a degree that it will lodge in your heart, words like the following from past presidents:

Ulysses Grant, 18th President

"Hold fast to the Bible as the sweet anchor of your liberties. Write its precepts in your hearts, and practice them in your lives. To the influence of this book are we indebted for all the progress made in true civilization, and to this we must look as our guide in the future. Righteousness exalteth a nation, but sin is a reproach to any people."

Benjamin Harrison, 23rd President

"If you take out of your statutes, your constitution, your family life all that is taken from the Sacred Book, what would there be left to bind society together?"

Ronald Reagan, 40th President

"Inside the Bible's pages lie all the answers to all of the problems man has ever known. It is my firm belief that the enduring values presented in its pages have a great meaning for each of us and for our nation. The Bible can touch our hearts, order our words, and refresh our souls.

The criteria for determining which historical facts will be omitted from textbooks and revised in the media and society as a whole seems to be any history that shows Christianity's influence on the Founding Fathers, on the Constitution and founding documents during America's birth, or on government itself, both state and federal. Such historical facts are sure to mention God, and that, according to the revisionists, would be a clear violation of "church and state separation," or perhaps more accurately, the separation of Christianity from every area of our society. Let's look at some examples of America's Christian history that would probably seem completely foreign to most students coming out of our universities today.

WASHINGTON WHO?

We'll begin with the words and beliefs of the people who founded this nation those 230-plus years ago. One of the great statements embodied in publications and documents is attributed to George Washington, America's first president. He said, *"It is impossible to rightly govern the world without God and the Bible."* Even in today's society, George Washington is a name that most people would know and be able to at least identify as our first president. A generation from now, however, that might be the only fact the majority will know.

One of the most amazing stories from Washington's history, first as a great military leader and then as president who served our country for forty-five years, was first told in a letter written by Washington to his wife Martha. I tell it here because it so dramatically portrays God's intervention and protection of a man whom God had destined to lead this country at the outset. In 1755, during the French and Indian War, Washington led thirteen-hundred troops in a battle against the Indians. When the battle was over, Washington remained in his saddle, the only officer that hadn't been shot. He later discovered four bullet holes in his uniform jacket, yet he did not have even a nick on him. He wrote to his wife and told her that God had protected him.

Fifteen years after that battle was fought, the old Indian chief who had led the party of Indians in battle against Washington's troops heard that Washington was in the area of the battleground, and traveled a good distance to see him. The chief told Washington that he had commanded his braves to concentrate on killing Washington, and had personally shot at him seventeen times "but 'twas all in vain, a power mightier far than we, shielded you! Seeing you were under the special guardianship of the Great Spirit, we immediately ceased to fire at you." He wanted to meet "the man that God wouldn't let die."[1]

This story is one of many that have been removed from school textbooks since the turn of the century. Why? It is an attempt to hide the fact that many of our Founding Fathers were in fact Christian men with a strong faith in God. Our liberal and godless education system would prefer to have students look to filthy-mouthed, drugged-up, rap music stars, and philandering pro-athletes for a role model than to one of the greatest men in history.

One of the lies that gained acceptance in the last half of the twentieth century, spread by haters of the "Religious Right" in America, is the claim that America was never a Christian nation, and was intended from its inception to be a melting pot of all religions with no preference for the religion of Christianity. This is patently false, and many of this nation's founders can argue the case for me. Patrick Henry, who was instrumental in the adoption of the Bill of Rights to amend the Constitution and five time Governor of Virginia, is probably best known for this statement: *"The appeal to arms and the God of hosts is all that is left us. But we shall not fight our battle alone. There is a just God that presides over the destinies of nations. The battle, sir, is not to the strong alone. Is life so dear or peace so sweet as to be purchased at the price of chains and slavery? Forbid it*

Almighty God. I know not what course others may take, but as for me, give me liberty, or give me death." (Patrick Henry, 1775)

He also said, *"It cannot be emphasized too strongly or too often that this great nation was founded, not by religionists, but by Christians, not by religions, but by the gospel of Jesus Christ."* (Patrick Henry, 1776)

America was not founded to unite all the religions of the world under one new humanist religion that prohibits any claim to absolute truth, and demands that differences be ignored. The Gospel of Jesus Christ was the ONLY religion in the minds of most Americans. So much was this the case, that religion was considered synonymous with Christianity in many of the founder's early writings.

America's sixth president, and the son of the second president, John Quincy Adams, wrote in 1860, *"The highest glory of the American Revolution was this: that it tied together in one indissoluble bond, the principles of civil government with the principles of Christianity."* It is Christianity, specifically, that our founders had in mind.

This view was upheld even by the first Chief Justice of the Supreme Court, John Jay. Jay, one of the three men most responsible for writing the U.S. Constitution, said, *"Province has given to our people the choice of their Rulers, and it is the duty, as well as the privilege and interest of our Christian nation, to select and prefer Christians for their Rulers."* It is this conviction that made our country great — a conviction that has been all but lost in the halls of government today, and was most assuredly expelled from the halls of justice long ago.

Today's justices need to be reminded of what former presidents and lawgivers had to say. Franklin Roosevelt, 32nd President, said, *"We cannot read the history of our rise and development as a nation without reckoning with the place the Bible has occupied in shaping the advances of the Republic. Where we have been the truest and most consistent to obey its precepts, we have attained the greatest measure of contentment and prosperity."*

FAITH IN CHRIST A GIVEN

The notion that America's leaders should be of the Christian faith was not merely the opinion of a few of the nation's founders, it was written into the constitutions of several states that a person must profess a faith in Jesus Christ to hold any state office. Maryland, for example, required an oath stating a belief in the Christian religion for every state officer. It was the belief of those who started this country that Christians would be better suited to uphold the laws of a Christian nation whose Constitution was first based on a belief in the God of the Bible. John Quincy Adams summed up this public sentiment when he said, *"All must admit that the reception of the teachings of Christ results in the purest patriotism, in the most scrupulous fidelity to public trust, and the best type of citizenship."*

Since 9/11, every election cycle brings with it another political argument over what it is to be patriotic. Barack Obama described patriotism, during the 2008 presidential election season, not as the wearing of a flag lapel pin in a display of one's pride in their country, but in NOT wearing that pin, and speaking out against the actions of his country.[2] Patriotism is no longer about taking pride in the generosity, decency, and good will of a people who have repeatedly spent blood and treasure around the world to help those less fortunate than ourselves. The Left would have us believe that patriotism can be summed up in a war protest, or a political sign waved in the face of a grieving widower to disparage the husband she lost in an "unjust war". We've come a long way indeed. For all his polished rhetoric, the forty-forth president's comments are disheartening, embarrassing, and often frightening.

While the Federal Government was prohibited from establishing a state religion by the establishment clause of the Constitution, this was never intended to, nor did it, place such restrictions on state and local governments. In fact, nine of the original thirteen colonies had official state churches. With a daily dose of "separation of church and state" being crammed down their throats, many school children today are being deprived of that which would inspire patriotism, love of country and loyalty to what its brave men and women have fought so valiantly to protect and preserve.

Our children today have been well schooled in the art of manipulating the legal system to get their way. Sadly, their parents often have thinner skin than their children, and a lawsuit is never far away when freedom of speech encompasses a religious topic. It wasn't always this way. In fact, the Bible was used as a textbook in every American classroom for over two-hundred years, in the form of The *New England Primer.* Published in the late 1600s, this textbook was the first reading primer designed for the New England colonies, and became the most successful and widely used textbook in American history. Used to instruct children in reading and grammar, many of the lessons were derived from the King James Bible and covered topics such as Christian morals, sin, and salvation through Christ. Until the beginning of the twentieth century, children in America learned to read by reading Bible stories, prayers, and Scripture from the Christian Bible.[3] Parents didn't file lawsuits, no nongovernmental organizations protested the use of Christian materials, and the courts were never asked to ban the Bible's use in public schools based on a constitutional requirement to keep church and state separate.

How could a country whose founders supposedly believed in an impregnable wall of separation between the states' business and anything religious let this go on for over two centuries? They did so because the founders of this country never intended to keep God out of public life, and certainly not out of public education. They expected the Bible to be a part of every child's education.

It is certainly worth noting that for the same reason the House and Senate reaffirmed Christianity's vital role in America's history and future in an 1853 report drafted by Congress following an investigation into religious influence in government. They did so because the founders expected Christianity to remain the religion of their descendants. Asked by a group of petitioners, who were against the co-mingling of religion and government, to separate Christian principles from government principles, the Congress of the United States waged a one year investigation of the matter in 1853. In 1854, the House Judiciary Committee reported, *"Had the people during the revolution, had any suspicion of any attempt to war against Christianity, that revolution would have been strangled in its cradle."* The report continued, *"At the time of the adoption of the Constitution and the Amendments, the universal sentiment was that Christianity should be encouraged, but not any one sect. In this age there can be no substitute for Christianity. That was the religion of the Founders of the Republic and they expected it remain the religion of their descendants. The great, vital and conservative element in our system is the belief of our people in the pure doctrines and the divine truth of the gospel of Jesus Christ."*[4] These are hardly the words of a government that believed Christianity was not to be the foundation upon which the republic was built, or that it should be kept separate from public and political life.

AMERICA'S SYMBOLS SAY IT ALL

In any culture, much can be gleaned about a people from their monuments, artwork, and architecture. America is no different, and it is obvious from the religious symbolism that permeates the national landscape that America was founded by Christians, and guided by Christian principles. The Washington Monument towers above the Washington D.C. skyline, and proclaims the words "Praise be to God." Inside the monument, inscriptions carry a message of praise in phrases such as "Holiness to the Lord," "Search the Scriptures," and "The memory of the just is blessed."

Within the halls of the Library of Congress are enshrined a Gutenberg Bible, and a display of a hand-copied Giant Bible of Mainz. Biblical inscriptions adorn the ceilings and walls of this great, historical building, and bear testimony of a society that once embraced the public display and reverence for the Holy Scriptures.

The Supreme Court of the United States displays a relief of Moses holding tablets upon which are written the Ten Commandments, an ironic display in light of the many lawsuits filed over the last decade in an attempt to ban the display of any religious symbolism on government property, in public schools, government buildings, public parks, and any other taxpayer-funded institutions. This demand, made by secular humanists who abhor freedom of speech when it is in conflict with their humanist belief system, is absurd when you consider the thousands of religious references on monuments and in government buildings all across the United States. The haters of all things Christian would have us erase historic inscriptions from the walls of the White House, remove Scripture verses that have long adorned the façade of Union Station, and throw out priceless religious paintings that decorate the rotunda of the Capital Building. Yet they will enlist the vast resources of the ACLU to fight for the right to display vile, anti-Christian artwork in our national art museums. Their hypocrisy is born out of a fear that the sheer volume of evidence for America's Christian heritage will expose their revisionist history for the lie that it is.

The artwork of a society can also reflect a great deal about the core values of a people. The volume of Christian art produced during the founding of this nation alone leads to only one conclusion. America was founded by believers in the God of the Bible, and their leaders felt no duty to hide that fact from public view, as our politicians and government bodies do today. Engravings and paintings of Moses or the Ten Commandments can be found not just in the Supreme Court building, but in many state and federal government buildings, including the White House. In the United States Capital building's chapel (yes, our founders saw no constitutional crisis in having a place of worship within a federal building), you will find a beautiful stained glass window depicting our first President, George Washington, kneeling in prayer.

In the White House you will find the ornate "Adam's Prayer Mantle" with the words "I pray heaven to bestow the best of blessings and all that shall heretofore inhabit it may none but honest and wise men ever rule under this roof," inscribed on the front.

In the rotunda of the Library of Congress, our national religious foundational ethic is artistically inscribed with the words, "One God, one law, and one far-off divine element to which the whole creation moves." The government that adorned their halls with such Christian artwork, Scripture, and words of faith believed that all creation, and especially all America, was created for one purpose — to live as Christians, govern according to God's Word, and live as a free people guided personally and collectively by the one true God and our Savior Jesus Christ. How far we have come from a country that proudly displayed their devotion to God in what they wrote, what they built, what they believed, the laws they lived by, and how they governed.

The artwork of a nation provides a window into the mind, heart, and soul of the people. For example, thirteenth century Italy was dominated by various sects of Christianity, and the art of the period reveals the total dominance of Christian thought. America was once as obviously Christian as thirteenth century Italy. Sadly, the art of our own times reveal a morally bankrupt society that would have been appalling to early Americans.

WARNING: RATED "R" FOR RIDICULOUS

The National Endowment for the Arts (NEA) basically operates as a system of welfare for the arts in the United States. Exorbitant grants are handed out for ridiculous purposes, and disguised as promoting the arts. Strange as it may seem to the average thinking American the NEA received stimulus money in the summer of 2009 that was somehow and in someway supposed to help our ailing economy. In 1996 the NEA awarded a $31,000 grant to stage a new play titled, *Corpus Christi*. This anachronistic play sets the Gospels in Texas during the fifties and sixties. A Christ figure, named Joshua in the play, attends Pontius Pilate High School and experiences the gay life when Judas approaches him at the senior prom. Scenes show Judas having gay relationships with classmates until he is finally betrayed, and dies on a cross as "The King of the Queers." These are your tax dollars at work.

At New York University (NYU), the NEA sponsored a performance by a Los Angeles Drag Queen named Vaginal Crème Davis. The perform-ance by Davis was sponsored by the NYU Queer Faculty Group. She supposedly acted as a psychic channel for a Gospel preacher named "Fornication, No! Theocracy, Yes!" This is considered art by our educa-tors today. Remember the grant that funded this performance when you fill out your tax return.

All of this was presaged by the outrageous display at the Whitney Museum of American Art in New York City of the "Piss Christ" statue. Andres Serrano placed a photograph of a crucifix in a jar of his own urine, and presented it to the art community as modern art. The NEA supported this magnificent artist with a $15,000 grant. As if that were not enough, the museum also exhibited a film showing a man pushing his head into another man's rectum, as well as Robert Mapplethorpe's "Self-Portrait", which featured a photograph of the artist with a bullwhip extruding from his rectum.

Gross, you say! Yes, America, this is the window into our society's mind, heart and soul provided by some of the artists of our day. Other examples could be cited, but would not be appropriate in a book of this nature, but they would make the above examples look like an elementary school art class. The world of art reflects the world of life, and the life reflected is that of corrupt and perverse minds. If Jesus does not return first, future generations might well look upon our artwork in their museums and history books, and wonder what kind of degenerates would display such vile, barbaric refuse in their galleries and places of learning.

It can sometimes seem our Christian heritage was so long ago and so brief as to have little meaning to a country over two centuries old. Our founders were undoubtedly men of God who founded this country on Christian principals, and their dreams and political ideology were continued perhaps longer than many American's might think. America's Christian heritage is not relegated to the first few pages of her history, or just to the Founding Fathers, or the first few presidents.

The decidedly Christian influence of America's leaders continued much later in America's history than secularists would like you to believe. Our twenty-sixth president, Theodore Roosevelt, assumed office in 1901 upon the assassination of President William McKinley and would serve until 1909. Late in Roosevelt's presidency, an observer recorded that the entire household at Oyster Bay, Roosevelt's presidential retreat on Long Island, observed the Sabbath. Not only could TR recite everything in the prayer book by heart, he sang every hymn as well. When asked his favorite hymns, he replied without hesitation, "How Firm a Foundation," and "Holy, Holy, Holy." An avid outdoorsman, woodsmen, and tennis player, TR refused to participate in any such activities on the Sabbath.[5] After his second term as president, and while still a relatively young man; TR delivered a series of lectures at the Pacific Theological Seminary in Berkeley, California in 1911. He devoted an entire address to *"The Bible and the Life of the People,"* as well as an entire address on the Eighth and Ninth Commandments.[6] The idea of a modern president giving moral and biblical lectures at a theological seminary following his presidency seems as remote a possibility today as a Martian landing in Manhattan and holding an evangelistic crusade. Such a display of Christian devotion would likely result in media analysts huddling together on every channel to discuss the president's overt religiosity, as if that were some kind of crime.

Just such a response was seen in the media criticism of George W. Bush following a 2004 election debate, when he was asked what philosopher had made the greatest impact on his life. To this, Bush simply answered, *"Jesus Christ."* Bush was mocked, criticized for offending other faiths, and the talking heads in the mainstream media debated the appropriateness of his statement for weeks. It didn't matter that the philosophy taught by Jesus had, in fact, had the most profound affect on Bush's life.

In 2009 when President Barack Obama was invited to address the Notre Dame graduates, their families and friends, media attention swirled around the invitation for weeks in advance mainly because of Obama's pro-abortion stance, a view at odds with the university's stated Catholic beliefs. But never mind, the powers-that-be prevailed and the president came. Once the event was over, the attention dissipated and little was made of the president's speech. This president offended few with his carefully crafted speech and usual expert performance. His message carried no heart-stirring, memorable Christian words of wisdom. It is a travesty at odds with what past presidents have said and done.

In today's media driven political climate, religion, and most especially Christianity, are taboo. Unless, of course, you're discussing Islam, the religion most responsible for terrorism and death around the globe, and then a dialogue about religion becomes acceptable. A dialogue about the Islamic faith is, they tell us, an important part of helping Americans understand that Islam is a religion of peace. It must be treated with respect and its adherents with sensitivity in a post 9/11 world. And, of course, not all Muslims are terrorists, a fact which Christians recognize. Members of the Christian faith, however, deserve no such special treatment. Instead, for the most part, Christianity is ridiculed by much of the media in particular. The bias is extreme, there is no balance. Except for Fox News, few, if any, TV talking heads respect or hold up for reverence the Christian lifestyle or point of view as being exemplary and worthy of discussion. It is entirely fair to state that the religion of Islam is portrayed in a positive light, while Christianity is denigrated and labeled intolerant for its claims to absolute truth.

It's been a little more than a hundred years since Roosevelt, a Christian president of unimpeachable character and sterling fidelity, led a nation that admired those very traits. We are getting exactly the kind of leadership we deserve in this day and age, because our leadership reflects the people we have become.

The evidence of America's purpose and her founder's original intent cannot be denied when one views this country's rich and well-preserved history. The mystery of America's greatness, throughout her relatively short history, is answered by the Founding Father's own words, of which we have been left so many.

I find these words, however, delivered in Washington's Inaugural Address to Both Houses of Congress, April 1789, to be especially meaningful: *"...it would be peculiarly improper to omit, in this first official act, my fervent supplications to that Almighty Being who rules over the universe, who presides in the councils of nations and whose providential aids can supply every human defect...that His benediction may consecrate to the liberties and happiness of the United States a Government instituted by themselves for these essential purposes; and may enable every instrument employed in its administration to execute with success, the functions allotted to his charge.*

"In tendering this homage to the Great Author of every public and private good, I assure myself that it expresses your sentiments not less than my own; nor those of my fellow-citizens at large, less than either...."[i]

President Roosevelt summarized America's purpose and strength perfectly when he said, *"America was born a Christian nation. America was born to exemplify that devotion to the elements of righteousness which are derived from the revelations of the Holy Scripture."*

We have strayed far from this devotion to that which is good and holy. Where we find ourselves now, how we got here, and whether America will survive the loss of her moral compass, and the abandonment of her reliance on God will be the topic of this book. We are balanced precariously on the precipice, and our choices going forward may lead to our destruction, alongside many of the great former world powers in history, if we do not act swiftly to restore our nation's conscience and standing before God. In the next chapter we will continue our journey with a tipping point in American history, when a blessed people first began to separate themselves from that which had made them great.

[**Note to the reader**: The material in this chapter is of major importance. You are well advised to take the time to read it carefully; it will inform you about things that have taken and are taking place, and you will gain an understanding so needed in today's political, cultural, and religious climate in our country.]

CHAPTER TWO
THE SEPARATION MYTH

*I tremble for my country when I
reflect that God is just, that His justice
cannot sleep forever.*

Thomas Jefferson
(In 1781, Jefferson made this statement in Query XVIII
of his Notes on the State of Virginia)

C hristians who placed the utmost importance in the freedom of every person to practice their religion founded America. However, they also saw America as a Christian nation, and they felt their highest duty was to found this nation on the Gospel of Jesus Christ, and see the Gospel message flourish. Sadly, over the course of the last half of the twentieth century and into the first decade of this new century, America has become a country determined to force upon all of us the right only to freedom FROM religion, rather than freedom OF religion. Humanism and its atheistic doctrines are fast becoming, if they have not already become the national religion for many, and the First Amendment has been rewritten, through judicial activism, to force Christianity underground and out of the public arena.

Whether it be lawsuits, court rulings, political correctness, or legislation that seeks to eliminate any signs of God and Christianity from the public arena, there can be no doubt that we are fast losing the very religious freedoms our Founding Fathers sought to guarantee under a new system of government in America. It is this attempt to remove God from our public lives and our society that has brought America to a tipping point in history.

THE BEGINNING OF THE EROSION OF RELIGIOUS FREEDOMS

How did we arrive at such a drastic transformation that would lead Supreme Court Justice Anthony Kennedy to describe the highest court in the land as more of a "National Theology Board" than a court of law?[1]

This erosion of our religious freedoms began with the Supreme Court's misuse of the phrase *"separation of church and state."* This phrase, repeated a thousand times by our peers, in the media, in our schools, and even in some of our more liberal Christian churches, is not to be found *in* the Constitution. That is right; it is not to be found even once. In fact, it is completely at odds with a literal reading of the First Amendment.

The First Amendment to the U.S. Constitution reads in part, "Congress shall make no law respecting an establishment of religion or prohibiting the free exercise thereof." It is obvious from a literal reading of this Amendment our founders intended it to apply to Congress, not the states, the education system, or any other governing body. It is also clear their intent was to restrict only the act of making a law. In other words, Congress, and Congress alone, would be prohibited from passing legislation that would establish a national religion, or infringe on our right to freely exercise our religion. Over 90 percent of our nation's founding fathers were Christians. Our forefathers saw Christianity and Christian Theism not as the enemy of Government, but as the foundation upon which a successful nation must be built.

NO DENOMINATION DOMINATION

When the Constitution was drafted, the religious debate held at the time was not a matter of whether to restrict government involvement in religion, or vice versa. The debate centered on a concern that one particular denomination of Christianity might one day gain favor among America's leaders, and be elevated, through legislation, to the status of a national religion, as had been the case in Europe. The first Amendment's intention was never intended to keep religion separate from all forms of government, or even to put all faiths on an equal footing, but to diminish rivalry within the Christian Church itself, and allow all Christians to worship freely without regulation by the Federal Government.

Justice Joseph Story, who served on the U.S. Supreme Court from 1811-1845, wrote that the framers of the Constitution generally believed that the state should encourage Christianity, as long as it did not interfere with individual freedom of worship. This belief remained the opinion of the courts for well over a century.[2]

REINTERPRETING THE FIRST AMENDMENT

Over time, it was the reinterpretation of the First Amendment that turned an attempt to level the playing field among Christian denominations into a government declaration of war on Christianity, with the judicial branch leading the charge. The first battle in that war was to reinterpret the First Amendment in such a way that its scope was no longer limited only to legislation from the U.S. Congress. Doing so requires not only a misinterpretation of the Establishment Clause, but requires one to ignore the second clause in the Amendment, which prohibits any infringement on our right to practice our religion freely.

When the American Civil Liberties Union (ACLU) files suit because a high school basketball team chooses to say a prayer before a game, *they* are violating the First Amendment's Free Exercise Clause by telling a United States citizen when and where they can pray. This is why those who believe in a separation of church and state focus in on the Establishment Clause, and prefer to ignore the Free Exercise Clause as if it contributes nothing to the Amendment's interpretation. Even then, a great deal of manipulation and misinterpretation was required by the courts to eventually apply the Establishment Clause to state and local governments, and broaden its scope to encompass anything religious in nature that can be even remotely connected to government funds or support.

To understand the Supreme Court's dramatic departure from the originally understood meaning of the First Amendment, it is helpful to first look at where, exactly, the phrase "separation of church and state" originated. Contrary to the evidentiary weight this phrase is often given, it is absent from the Constitution, and appeared in only two court cases during the first 150 years of the Supreme Court's history.[3] The stark fact is the phrase was plucked from a letter written by Thomas Jefferson to the Danbury Baptist Association in 1803. Justice Hugo Black, in the case Everson v. Board of Education, would woefully misinterpret this statement in a landmark decision. We will deal with Everson v. Board of Education in more detail later, but I first want to examine the history behind the phrase that the Supreme Court cites as proof that the founders intended to create a wall of separation between church and state.

Too often, defenders of the "separation of church and state" myth are unwilling to cite the letter they use to defend their position in context, and with the appropriate relevant historical background. It suits their defense better to simply state that Jefferson coined the phrase, giving it credibility, and then fill in the blanks with an intended meaning that makes no sense, especially coming from Thomas Jefferson.

Jefferson's letter was penned in response to an inquiry made by the Danbury Baptist Association regarding the First Amendment. The Danbury Baptists believed strongly in church autonomy, and it was a sermon on this topic, titled "The Garden in the Wilderness," given by Roger Williams, that led to the dialogue found in the correspondence with Jefferson. The sermon given by Williams explained that the purpose of civil government is to allow religion to flourish, not to regulate it. Jefferson's response to this sentiment was an expression of his agreement with the Baptists intended to reassure them that he, too, believed the federal government must not regulate religion. What follows is the portion of Jefferson's letter that gave birth to a mythical wall of separation, and used by the courts to apply restrictions on the practice of one's religion, while requiring that the states enforce them. (The emphasis in bold is mine.)

> *"Believing with you that religion is a matter which lies solely between man and his God, that he owes account to none other for his faith or his worship, that the **legislative powers of government** reach actions only, and not opinions, I contemplate with sovereign reverence that act of the whole American people which declared that their **legislature***

should make no law respecting an establishment of religion, or prohibiting the free exercise thereof, thus building a wall of separation between church and State. Adhering to this expression of the supreme will of the nation in behalf of the rights of conscience, I shall see with sincere satisfaction the progress of those sentiments which tend to restore to man all his natural rights, convinced he has no natural right in opposition to his social duties."

It is obvious to any objective person that Jefferson was speaking of the federal government, and not the governments of each state, school board, government office, or any other publicly funded entity other than Congress. Jefferson believed that the First Amendment applied to the Legislative Branch, and intended in this letter to reassure a group of Baptist preachers that the Legislative Branch of government would not make it their business to establish a national church, and regulate the religious affairs of the people as had happened in Europe.

By the way, it is helpful for one to know something of the religious conflicts in Europe prior to our nation's birth. Those who wish to ban religion from the public square have completely twisted Jefferson's intentions, and would have us believe people of faith are constitutionally forbidden from exercising their religion freely when they enter the realm of government and politics, or even indirectly utilize public funding. The wall of separation Jefferson described was never intended to ban Christians from government, but rather to ban the federal government from legislating matters of faith and religion. The courts not only turned the wall around, they used Jefferson's "wall of separation" to impose the First Amendment on the STATES. This is important, and we will explore how they arrived at this expansion of the Bill of Rights as we go along.

It's also relevant to the debate to point out that the courts used the words and opinions of a man who had absolutely nothing to do with the writing of the First Amendment, and wasn't even present for the debates that led to the writing of the Constitution and subsequent Amendments. At the time the Bill of Rights was being debated, and during the movement to ensure freedom of religion in America, Jefferson was serving as Ambassador to France. His only connection with the homeland and what was taking place there came through letters from his associates back home. The letter to the Danbury Baptists wasn't even written until a decade after the Bill of Rights was ratified.[4]

JEFFERSON'S OPINION OF RELIGION

However, Jefferson did have his own opinion on religion, and its place in government and society. He did not write his letter to the Baptists in a societal vacuum. A much clearer and defensible picture of Jefferson's views on religious freedom is easily gleaned from the views and opinions he expressed in writing and deed during his presidency. For example, just one year after Jefferson wrote his letter to the Danbury Baptists, he made a treaty with the Kaskaskia Indians wherein he agreed to use federal funds to build them a Roman Catholic Church, and even pay the salaries of the church's priests with federal dollars. Obviously, Jefferson did not feel that using federal funds to build houses of worship violated the Constitution. Jefferson must have believed that the establishment clause applied only to the actual establishment of a national religion through Congressional legislation, just as the amendment clearly states.

Jefferson also saw no conflict with the Constitution when he extended, no less than three times, an act signed by George Washington to appropriate land for the "Society of the United Brethren for propagating the Gospel among the Heathen."[5] Does this sound like the actions of a man who believed that there must be a wall of separation, high and impregnable, between church and state? Obviously not! His actions clearly indicate that he not only did not believe the First Amendment applied to the states, but he also did not believe the First Amendment mandated an absolute ban on any involvement in religion by the federal government.

Sadly, the courts ignored Jefferson's words when they did not fit their purpose of expanding judicial power, and silencing people of faith. Jefferson imparted sage advice to all future judges in 1823 when he instructed Justice William Johnson, "On every question of construction, carry ourselves back to the time when the Constitution was adopted, recollect the spirit manifested in the debates, and instead of trying what meaning may be squeezed out of the text, or invented against it, conform to the probable one in which it was passed."[6]

Even then, Jefferson knew that the judicial system had the potential to become a dictatorship, legislating themselves into a position of unconstitutional power through judicial activism. He once said of the judiciary, "The Constitution is a mere thing of wax in the hands of the judiciary, which they may twist and shape into any form they please."[7] If he only had known just how much they would twist his own words, and what they would squeeze out of them, I am positive he would be sickened.

JUDICIAL REVIEW: THE DANGER WITHIN

The court's revision and misrepresentation of the First Amendment, and what our founders intended the Constitution to mean, is an egregious abuse of power that should not have been allowed to stand. However, it was an even more despotic decision by the Supreme Court that gave them the power to affect such change. In 1803, the courts fulfilled Jefferson's prophecy that predicted their eventual corrupting influence on the Constitution by ruling into law the doctrine of Judicial Review. This new doctrine led Jefferson to respond, "To consider the judges as the ultimate arbiters of all constitutional questions [is] a very dangerous doctrine indeed, and one which would place us under the despotism of an oligarchy. The Constitution has erected no such single tribunal, knowing that to whatever hands confided, with the corruptions of time and party, its members would become despots. It has more wisely made all the departments co-equal and co-sovereign within themselves."

Jefferson was speaking of the decision in Marbury v. Madison in which the Supreme Court gave to itself the power to ignore the will of the people and the vote of our representative government, by declaring that the court has the authority to review all legislation and determine its constitutionality. This doctrine became known as Judicial Review. Judicial Review gives the federal courts the power to consider or overturn any congressional and state legislation, or other official governmental action deemed inconsistent with the Constitution, Bill of Rights, or federal law.[8] Simply defined, the courts can overturn the people's majority vote either by overturning a majority vote in the Congress that we elect, or by overturning laws enacted by state and local governing bodies, or laws passed by referendum. They, in effect, made themselves kings, and gave themselves power over the executive and legislative branch that they were never intended to have.

Since Marbury v. Madison, nine unelected judges have held the power to control every aspect of public policy, and dictate to the other branches of government what legislation they may or may not pass and enact. From that moment to the present, we have been and are being ruled over by an oligarchy that can change and has changed all of our lives in an instant.

Nevertheless, they did not stop there. As was mentioned earlier, the Supreme Court further shifted the balance of power to the Judicial Branch in 1925 when, in Gitlow v. New York, they ruled that the Bill of Rights applied not just to the Federal government, as it had always been, but applied to the States as well. Ignoring precedent set by their predecessors, the court ruled that the Fourteenth Amendment extended the Bill of Rights to the States. The Fourteenth Amendment was one of several post Civil War Amendments, written to define what constituted citizenship, and to extend this right to black people and freed slaves. It includes a clause granting due process and equal protection under the law to all people in a state's jurisdiction. The courts used this language to rule that the Bill of Rights must apply to the states to meet the requirements of the "Due Process" clause. The case itself dealt with a freedom of speech and the press issue, and the courts ruling allowed the Federal Government to enforce laws regarding these freedoms, instead of leaving enforcement with the states as originally intended, and had been until that point. It would not be long before the courts would violate the original meaning of Jefferson's "separation of church and state" terminology and allow the federal government to enforce laws on matters of religion as well.

In 1940, using the same argument, the Supreme Court ruled that the "free exercise" clause of the First Amendment also applied to the states. The

Federal Government was then given the very power that Jefferson had sought to reassure the Danbury Baptists it would not claim for itself. In direct opposition to the Constitution, the historical record, and the founder's belief that religion was to be a matter for the states to regulate, the courts began the process of turning Jefferson's wall of separation around.

In 1947, The Supreme Court's ruling in Everson v. Board of Education solidified this judicial intrusion into religious affairs, and made "separation of church and state" the law of the land by, once again, applying the First Amendment's Establishment Clause to the states.

Everson v. Board of Education was not unlike some of the court cases we see being filed by the ACLU today. A New Jersey school district was lawfully using tax dollars to pay for students' transportation to and from school. The problem arose when a taxpayer named Arch R. Everson filed suit against the school board for using public funds to reimburse students for transportation to and from Catholic parochial schools. Everson argued that this constituted government aid to religion. The case went all the way to the Supreme Court, with Everson losing his case in the lower courts, and finally in 1947, via Justice Hugo Black, the court handed down the ruling, which confirmed that the use of state funds for transportation to religious schools was in fact constitutional. However, the courts ruling also included opinions that drastically reinterpreted the Establishment Clause of the First Amendment. The opinion read, "Neither a state nor the Federal Government can set up a church. Neither can pass laws, which aid one religion, aid all religions or prefer one religion over another... No tax in any amount, large or small, can be levied to support any religious activities or institutions, whatever they may be called, or whatever form they may adopt to teach or practice religion. Neither a state nor the Federal Government can, openly or secretly, participate in the affairs of any religious organizations or groups and vice versa."[9]

In one court decision, the First Amendment was turned upside down. States had for over a century and a half not only established state churches in some cases, but passed laws dealing with religious matters, and as was covered in the last chapter, even required a belief in Jesus in order to hold office. If it were unconstitutional for the states to involve themselves in religious matters in any way, and if the Federal Government truly had the right to apply the First Amendment to the states, rather than just to Congress, as it is written, then why did no Supreme Court ever put an end to the unconstitutional co-mingling of religion and state in nearly every state in the union up to that point? Why did the founders remain silent, and allow the states to continue their influence and participation in church affairs?

The courts and the federal government were silent because they intended for the states to act as a representative government representing the people, not Washington, and the restrictions placed on the federal government were never meant to apply to the states. The only other possible explanation is that every judge, politician, president, and most citizens for the first 150 years of America's history, as well as the authors of the Constitution themselves, didn't have a clue what the First Amendment was intended to mean, or how it was to be enforced. Jefferson's second Inaugural Address delivered March 14, 1805, however, indicates that they knew very well what both clauses of the First Amendment were intended to accomplish. While addressing the nation, he said, *"In matters of religion, I have considered that its free exercise is placed by the Constitution independent of the powers of the General (federal) Government. I have therefore undertaken on no occasion to prescribe the religious exercises suited to it, but have left them, as the Constitution found them, under the direction and discipline of the church or **state authorities** acknowledged by the several religious societies."*

Notice that Jefferson did not say he would leave religious matters "under the direction of the courts or the Federal Government." Quite the opposite, he placed them with the church and state authorities, where the Constitution dictates they should be. The same man credited with giving us the law of Separation of Church and State obviously believed that state and local governments were in no way restricted by the establishment clause from involvement in religious affairs.

It was the opinion of our founders and the nation that the free exercise of religion was never to be impeded by government, and should in fact be encouraged and supported. The 1892 case Holy Trinity v. United States further supports this fact as revealed by the opinion of Supreme Court Justice David Josiah Brewer. The crux of the case was to determine whether a statute banning the payment of relocation costs for foreign workers could be applied to the importation of Christian ministers. America's Christian identity was presented as the strongest support for the court's conclusion. Justice Brewer used nearly half of the opinion to establish that America is a Christian nation, in order to demonstrate that Congress could not have meant for this statute to apply to Christian ministers. He understood what previous justices had known — that the founders would not have condoned nor supported the current law of Separation of Church and State as applied today.

CONFUSED COURTS, MISGUIDED JUDGES

In the decades since the Judicial Branch's all-out assault on the First Amendment, the Supreme Court has been ruling on religious issues and establishing legal precedent that further deteriorates our religious freedoms, which in today's court system is the equivalent of passing legislation. Although, our representative government has never passed a law mandating the separation of church and state, we increasingly see our churches and our personal spirituality being regulated, restricted, and generally interfered with by the courts. No more proof is needed than the religious entanglement constantly present in our courts to prove that the judicial system has usurped the legislative branches power to make laws, and destroyed any balance of powers that might have existed when this country was founded. They continue to make laws restricting the American people from freely exercising their religion, and we have seemingly been powerless to do anything about it.

We have no power to affect change through our state governments, regardless of whom we elect, because the federal government has the power to overturn state legislation through the courts. We can elect representatives to Congress who share our disdain for the practice of legislating from the bench, but thus far, they have been unwilling to challenge the court's abuse of power. Perhaps they feel it is unwise to challenge those who have the power to veto any legislation they might pass, with one majority decision. This is a serious problem when even the President's veto can be overridden by two-thirds of the Congress, yet a tribunal of unelected judges can overrule both of them, and remain the final word on what laws we are forced to live under.

We find ourselves closer and closer to that very government our founders fled when they left Europe in order to practice their religion in freedom, without government intrusion. The only difference being, instead of one King, we now have nine. As we will see in the next chapter, the courts have used their power, with the help of anti-Christian civil rights groups like the ACLU, to ban God from our classrooms and strip our children of their right to worship their God freely in public.

CHAPTER THREE
TAKEOVER OF AMERICA'S CLASSROOMS

*We can't all be CEOs [Chief Executive
Officers]. But any of us can be a salty
influence in an area of even more lasting
influence: our children's schools.*

Charles Colson

in *Being the Body: A New Call for the Church to be
Light in the Darkness*

One moment Cassie Bernall was reading her Bible in her Colorado high school classroom, and moments later she was crouched under a table sobbing and crying out, "Dear God. Dear God. Why is this happening? I just want to go home." Cassie was taken home, but not to her loving parents who had witnessed her acceptance of Christ and the dramatic change that had taken place in her troubled life. Cassie went to her heavenly home and Savior when she was shot in the head by one of the Columbine killers.

Another student, who lay wounded on the cafeteria floor, was overheard praying for God's help when she was asked by one of the gunman, "Do you believe in God?" She replied, "Yes, I do." The killer said, "Why?" as he turned to continue the mass slaughter of innocent children in what became the worst school shooting in U.S. history. Since that dreadful day countless numbers of tragic school shootings have taken place across this nation. Places come to mind like Virginia Tech University where thirty-three were shot to death. Nickel Mines, PA where ten young girls were shot killing five and the list goes on. (Please see the Appendix for a listing of world-wide school shootings since 1996.)

Such a juxtaposition of cultures underscores the crisis in the nation's classrooms. Spiritual emptiness, a toxic society, and family instability all undermine what happens in the elementary and secondary classrooms of America, with its tentacles now in colleges and universities across the country. Public schools no longer teach the importance of character, morality, and respect for human life.

What brought us to this place of such utter spiritual darkness where we would see a child hold enough hatred and rage in his heart to obliterate the lives of his fellow students? The corruption of the minds of our children can be traced to the removal of God from the classroom. When our government, our courts, and academic philosophy kicked God out of the classroom, it caused a societal and cultural shift that we are paying for even now, and will continue to pay for, unless Christians take back their country and fight for their children's right to live a life, both at home and at school, that is pleasing to God.

The process of kicking God out of our schools, as with so many other modern social ills, began in the courts. The first step in ushering God out of the classroom was to ban children from talking to Him. In 1962, the Supreme Court deemed state-sponsored prayer unconstitutional in New York Public schools in Engel v. Vitale, and imposed on our children the first of many "thought crimes" that would fill American jurisprudence.

A little history about how and why that action came is in order. In the 1950s the New York Board of Regents, a group appointed by the State Legislature to oversee New York schools, had recommended a plan for moral education within the school system. Part of that plan included a daily prayer. After some debate, local religious leaders reached a compromise on the wording of the prayer to be recited by the students each morning. The wording of the prayer uses language similar to that found in so much of America's early history. In fact, it could actually be viewed as a concise summary of the religious phrases and petitions to God found on our money, in our National Anthem, engraved on our court buildings, and in the text of countless Inaugural Addresses and speeches given by our elected leaders for decades. It simply read "Almighty God, we acknowledge our dependence upon Thee, and we beg Thy blessings upon us, our parents, our teachers and our country." The prayer would have the same meaning if it read, "In God We Trust" (on U.S. currency), and "God Bless America" (a quote found nearly everywhere and repeated to this day by nearly every politician in the country).

The regents were well aware that religion had been the target of many lawsuits aimed at defining the First Amendment's intended scope, and they went out of their way to avoid problems by making the prayer optional. Each school board and the parents decided whether the prayer was to be used or not. Thus, a decision that deemed the prayer unconstitutional would in effect, be telling students, schools, and parents that they could not choose to pray in school. Most of the New York City school districts shunned the new plan, and other Districts followed their lead. Since the Supreme Court had already ruled in the 1948 case, McCollum v. Board of Education, that any religious instruction in public schools was unconstitutional, fear and intimidation had already made many Christians afraid to practice their religion in such a way.

In 1958 five parents in New Hyde Park, Long Island, filed the inevitable lawsuit. The parents believed the regent's prayer violated the establishment clause, because their children were being forced to pray, which wasn't true because each of them could be excused from participating. None other than the ACLU funded the parents' suit in large part. At first, their efforts met with defeat when lower courts ruled that it was not a violation of the First Amendment, and instead offered remedies that included enacting policies to eliminate embarrassment among those who opted out of the prayer. Thus was born the first generation of whiners, who believed the Constitution guaranteed them a right to never be offended, never suffer embarrassment, and never have to hear anything they didn't like, even if someone else's rights had to be trampled in order to make this happen.

The New York Appellate Division, as well as the State Court of Appeals ruled against the parents stating that the nation's founders had designed the Establishment Clause to prohibit adopting an official religion, or favoring a particular religion, and could not have meant to prohibit a mere profession of belief in God. Federal and State authorities had been doing this very thing for decades, and encouraging others to do the same with no argument from the courts until well into the twentieth century. The School Board defended the prayer citing the free exercise clause, and successfully won several appeals by maintaining that the prayer was an example of the students freely exercising their religion, and it in no way established a religion.

Thus it was that on June 25, 1962, their luck changed when the Supreme Court ruled by a nearly unanimous vote that the prayer was unconstitutional. Justice Hugo Black again ruled against freedom of religion, and cited in his opinion the bitter rivalry between England and colonial America, and a supposed belief among Americans at the time that the co-mingling of church and state matters was dangerous. This was a claim that cannot be supported by the historical record, and reflects a general hostility toward religion on the part of Justice Black. Black seemed to anticipate the backlash that would surely come from his decision when he wrote in his defense it was "neither sacrilegious nor antireligious to say that each separate government in this country should stay out of the business of writing or sanctioning official prayers and leave that purely religious function to the people themselves and to those the people choose to look to for religious guidance."[1] What Black didn't seem to understand was that the court was taking away the people's right to sanction, or even recite prayers, thereby telling them who they could and could not look to for religious guidance. It was dishonest of Black to claim he was leaving matters of prayer in the hands of the people, when in fact he was creating legal precedent that would see the government regulating prayer for certain groups of people. Engel v. Vitale was just the first in a long line of decisions that would effectively ban any prayer, including voluntary prayer, in all public schools in America.

NO GOD, NO RULES:
THE BEGINNING OF THE CULTURAL SHIFT

As early as the 1960s, such rulings against religion began to have a profound affect on the lives of religious, and especially Christian Americans. One Fort Worth, Texas public school teacher was reprimanded for having a Bible just laying on her desk, even though there was never so much as a reference to the Bible during class. Before 1963, most public schools had both Bible reading and prayer on the public address system of the schools. Each morning students heard a reading from the Word of God, and heard a student lead the school in prayer. All of that changed virtually overnight, with the Madelyn Murray O'Hare Supreme Court decision. In 1960, O'Hare, who later founded the group "American Atheists," cemented the Engel decision in legal precedent, filing a suit on behalf of her son, claiming it was unconstitutional for the Baltimore City public school system to require him to read from the Bible. Her suit was later joined with another lawsuit that had been filed over the issue of prayer in school, and it finally reached the Supreme Court in 1963. The court sided with O'Hare in an eight to one decision, effectively banning prayer in public schools, and forbidding the recitation of Bible verses in public schools.

With children effectively silenced when it came to their right to communicate with their Creator, the courts moved on to the Word of God, which had been used as a textbook in American schools since the first colonies were founded. God had officially been expelled from the American education system, and the atheists had won. O'Hare's victory brought about a cultural shift in our society felt around the country. The mere mention of God in a government building or school became taboo, and our school systems began what would be a devastating decline into moral depravity, failing grades, and a rise in crime rates among children. We took the Ten Commandments off the walls and put metal detectors in the halls! By 1985, the courts would even go so far as to ban a moment of silence in school, during which children were allowed to meditate, pray, or simply sit quietly and think. Those who demand a right to freedom FROM religion and religious people saw as a threat even the possibility that someone might communicate silently and privately with a higher being of their choosing.

WHEN THE BIBLE WAS EXPELLED FROM OUR SCHOOLS

One of the most striking correlations between the absence of God and the decline of education in America was seen in the immediate decline of SAT scores beginning the very year the O'Hare case was decided, and has continued for decades. Many veteran teachers trace the loss of behavioral control in public schools directly to the changed atmosphere when the Bible was expelled from school.

Considering the history that led to the founding of a Christian nation so moored in the teachings of the Bible, it is astounding to see the dramatic cultural shift that has taken place when our current attitude toward the Bible is contrasted with that of our ancestors. Shakespeare and Milton, Bunyan and Browning, Sir Walter Scott and Robert Burns — the greatest names in literary history — abounded with references to the Bible that were understood by their readers. The average Victorian man knew as much about the Bible as the average Joe-Six-Pack knows about the sports pages today. When the courts took the Word of God from our classrooms, they extinguished the bright light of liberty that was once our beacon of hope, and destroyed the very soul of our great nation. It was a travesty being repeated around the globe in civilized societies that had once made Christianity the bedrock of their governments, their families, and their lives.

THE ATTACK ON SCRIPTURE AS GOD'S WORD

The roots of America's loss of the Bible sink deep into the soil of the period in western history called the *Enlightenment*. This eighteenth century intellectual and cultural movement first subjected the Bible to harsh critical treatment. The Bible began to be examined as if it were just any other book. By the nineteenth century, radical biblical criticism had invaded the German university systems and spilled over into England and America. Liberal scholars denied that Moses wrote the first five books of the Old Testament and that Paul wrote all of the thirteen letters attributed to him in the New Testament. Cynical professors first found historical support for two books of Isaiah, and then three! Peter did not write 2 Peter, and the Gospels were a hodgepodge of sources pasted together by the ancient church, which invented the words and put them into the mouth of Jesus Christ.

"EXPENDABLE MYTHS"

By the mid-twentieth century, scholars such as Rudolph Bultmann at the University of Marburg proclaimed the Gospels had to be demythologized. Bultmann believed modern men and women would never accept the miraculous elements in the Gospels and deemed them expendable myths at any rate. This heretical view of the Bible spilled from the universities into the seminaries. Soon the major liberal Protestant pulpits were filled with preachers who were filled with doubt concerning the veracity of the Word. Loss of confidence in the pulpit led to loss of belief in the pew. The domino theory of theological decline proved true. This devastating domino effect moved from the university and toppled into the seminaries, from the seminaries into the pulpits, and from the pulpits it has crashed into the pews. Everyone has lost.

LIBERAL ELITISM: THE POSSIBILITY OF A GLOBAL UTOPIA

Alongside this development, another theological movement began in the nineteenth century, connected with the name Schleiermacher. According to the famous theologian, religious *feelings* are what really matter. If a given biblical text makes you *feel* spiritual, that is the Word of God to you. This led to the so-called "Dalmatian Theology" — the Bible is inspired in spots, and I am inspired to pick the spots. Of course, if the Seventh Commandment or the Malachite command to tithe does not feel good to me, it is not the Word of God to me. How convenient! All of this is akin to the "New Testament" edited by the deistic Thomas Jefferson. Jefferson liked the moral teachings of Christ, but even he was skeptical of the miracles or other teachings he considered unworthy. Jefferson cut up and pasted together his own New Testament with sayings that did not offend his rationalistic mind. This sentimental and rationalistic approach to the Bible has come to characterize a great many Americans.

An out of control Judicial System, and this new tolerant age of liberal elitism have left us with a society that mocks the Bible that they know absolutely nothing about. There's a rampant disdain for biblical absolutes in a world that believes being enlightened means successfully blurring the lines between good and evil. This, they reason, is the sophisticated approach to creating a global Utopia. If moral values are made the antiquated philosophy of unenlightened Bible-thumpers, then we can declare victory and call ourselves officially evolved. This atmosphere of hostility toward religion, coupled with a lack of respect for the Bible, has led even Christians to accept a watered-down Gospel based on self-help books and "Scripture for Dummies". Students learn from a very early age that the Bible contains hate-speech, and outdated intolerant views that are incompatible with pop culture, and are too offensive to lure new converts. While they may learn something about the religion of their parents from Sunday school teachers and the occasional sermon they stopped text messaging long enough to listen to, they are woefully uneducated in Christian doctrine and biblical truths. Most of them can't even explain their faith, let alone defend it.

A CASE IN POINT

If anyone should know the Bible, one would expect that incoming students at Wheaton College would know at least the core doctrinal points found in any Christian Church's statement of beliefs. The brightest and best from the evangelical world enter that famed Illinois college. Yet, when incoming freshmen were asked to place in biblical order the story of Abraham, the Old Testament Prophets, the Crucifixion, and Pentecost, one-third of these young adults from the heart of evangelical Protestantism could not put these events in the proper sequence. Half of the respondents did not know that the Christmas story was in Matthew, and the Passover story was in Exodus.[2]

At Baylor University, the world's largest Baptist University, a student who was asked the definition of an epistle answered, "An epistle is the wife of an apostle." Another student wrote a long essay on the Parable of the Sower, making up a story about a man who had a terrible "sore" that Jesus healed — a comment on Baptist spelling as well as biblical knowledge.

These examples indicate that the Bible has become honored in general but not in particular. Dr. R. G. Lee, the famed Memphis, Tennessee pastor, used to warn, "sermonettes by preacherettes make Christianettes." Today's emphasis on Church-Lite with twenty minute feel-good therapy sessions has yielded a world of biblical illiteracy. The Bible may be lofted in the preacher's hand from the pulpit, but the presence of studied exegetical preaching is now rare in the land. One noted expository preacher stated, "I am brought into churches like an antique, and put on display so that people can see how it used to be done." When preachers use everything from comic strips to sitcom episodes as texts, is it little wonder that people have forgotten the Bible? Ultimately, the people in the pew will reflect the attitude of the man in the pulpit when it comes to reverence for the Word of God.

Many in the academic community consider the very term "Christian intellectual" an oxymoron. Many Christians have an obvious lack of knowledge about their own Book of Scripture which likely doesn't help their image much among those who are trained to debate, for instance, the "scientific" evidence for the theory of evolution beginning in grade school. With society's increasingly cynical opinion of Scripture, unfounded skepticism about the accurate transmission and relevancy of a two thousand-year-old book, the self-anointed "great thinkers" of our time look down their collective noses at people of faith, and immediately denounce any contribution they might make to the academic community as the ravings of religious zealots who haven't evolved to their higher level of consciousness with the rest of society.

THE BIAS AGAINST THE CHRISTIAN FAITH IN ACADEMIA: THE ONE RELIGION EVERYONE LOVES TO HATE

Needless to say, there is a bias against the Christian faith in academia that borders on the fanatical. One African American ministerial student in California complained that every world religion received a warm evaluation in his secular History of Religion class, except Christianity, which was roundly ridiculed and dismissed as absurd. This experience has been repeated *ad nauseum* to the scandal of Christian students everywhere. Half-educated professorial wannabe's, who have never so much as read the great Christian theologians and philosophers, much less the Bible, revile a faith they know only in caricature.

The television networks replay video of the brainwashing that passes for education in Moslem Madras's across the Middle East. In these Islamic schools, groups like the Taliban indoctrinate the next generation with ignorance and hate. This is a horrible fate for the young men in such pseudo-institutions. Yet there is something just as tragic in the American educational sphere. Diplomas are given to students who cannot name the four Gospels, have no concept of the rudiments of Christianity, and at the same time ridicule the very thing they do not know. The writings of Augustine, Thomas Aquinas, Luther, Calvin — not to mention Barth and Brunner — are considered off limits in the development of the American student's mind. Our institutions graduate technocrats with empty hearts, MBAs who can run companies, but not their own lives, and lawyers who can argue before judges, but have no fear of the Judge who one day will decide their own eternal fate.

Meanwhile, those schools that seek to maintain even a semblance of the Christian faith face the scorn of the academy, and lawsuits brought by their own professors. A former president of Baylor University, Dr. Robert Sloan, faced harassment from his own faculty, and the financial and professional burden of a lawsuit because of his insistence upon the Baylor faculty having a Christian testimony. If this is what educated professionals must endure in a former denominational school, what must persecution be like in the secular academy with no Christian influence whatsoever? We are producing generations of students with little or no concept of the Christian mind, even in the abstract. While they are fed the fodder of multi-culturalism, they never encounter the writings, for instance, of C. S. Lewis as a lay theologian, one of the mighty pens of the twentieth century. As a result, Christianity has become the one religion that everyone loves to hate. It is the only spiritual path that cannot be tolerated, most especially by the very people who preach tolerance and acceptance among the faiths.

Christianity is openly demonized in school curriculums while Christians are relentlessly pursued through the legal system. This can be seen no more frequently and viciously than in our education system. Sadly, our children are an easy target for their peers and their teachers, because too often they don't have the biblical or historical knowledge to defend themselves. They hear day after day that their religion is intolerant, divisive, and a fraud. Is it any wonder? Often their parents are no more capable of defending the Bible than they are? When little Johnny faces an atheist classmate, steeped in the dogma of Charles Darwin, he finds himself woefully unprepared to explain his belief in a seven day creation. He may never have been told how the Bible's historical, archaeological, and prophetic accuracy give him a ready defense of his beliefs. Additionally, he has most likely not been taught by his parents or the church that there exists an abundance of scientific proof for a young earth -- created, flooded, restored, and saved by the God of the universe. Far too many churches avoid such controversial topics as prophecy, creationism, and the translation and transmission of the Bible. So, Christian students, parents, and teachers are ridiculed, mocked, and may even find themselves subjected to litigation.

If you don't believe that Christians are being systematically silenced and persecuted in our schools and universities today, you haven't been reading or watching the news. It also may be the case that people have become so accustomed to discrimination against Christians, it no longer registers as a violation of a person's rights. The religious right in this country have been demonized. It has become almost automatic for non-Christians, and some Christians, to suspend their strongly held belief in freedom of speech when words like Christ, and Jesus hit their ears and they realize their right to never ever be offended has been violated. Suddenly they have no problem discriminating based solely on a person's religious viewpoint, and the free exchange of ideas makes way for censorship.

A quick search of the Internet for the words "Christianity banned in school" will deliver to your monitor 8,590,000 hits as of this writing. That's million! If you scroll through the links, you will find court case, after court case, all targeting Christians for simply making their religion a visible part of their lives.

In Phoenix, Arizona, the Alliance Defense Fund filed a suit after Maricopa Unified School District refused to allow a church to distribute its fliers announcing its Awana 2004 Bible Study program to students.[3] The district allows non-profit organizations to distribute literature, but only if they do not contain any religious content. They do this even though the Supreme Court has ruled repeatedly that prohibiting religious groups from taking part in an open forum, while allowing all non-religious nonprofits to participate, is a clear violation of the First Amendment. Those who support an absolute separation of church and state have been arguing for decades that government cannot treat one religion more favorably than another religion. Yet, they fail to see the hypocrisy inherent in treating people or groups with non-religious viewpoints more favorably than those with religious viewpoints.

Yet, another Christian student was denied his religious freedom at a Wisconsin high school. The student's teacher instructed each student to draw a landscape picture as an assignment for her art class. When one particular student handed in a landscape drawing that featured a road, clouds, mountains, and a cross in the background along with the words "John 3:16 — A sign of love," the teacher demanded that he remove the scriptural reference, or cover it with a border. Apparently, the teacher had required that each student sign a document at the beginning of the school year agreeing not to use any depictions of blood, violence, sexual connotations, or religious beliefs in their art work. When the student protested the censorship of religious symbols, the teacher informed him that he had "signed away his First Amendment rights." He refused to remove the cross from his picture, and was given a zero for the assignment.[4]

In the first place, it is utterly disgusting that a Bible verse that the majority of Americans have memorized at some point in their life would be so offensive to anyone. This fact is made even more stunningly ridiculous by the fact that pictures including demonic illustrations were allowed to remain unchanged, and were not graded down for their content. The teacher had no problem with symbols of Satanism being included in her student's work, but the religion practiced by the vast majority of the American people was deserving of censorship. As the Senior Legal Counsel for Alliance Defense Fund David Cortman said, "A public school cannot require students to sign away their constitutional right to free speech and religious expression, nor are they permitted to censor Christian religious expression in artwork while at the same time allowing other types of religious depictions." That may be, but cases like this one are happening in schools across this country on a daily basis and school systems are running scared.

You might think that places of higher learning would be more open to the free exchange of ideas, but you'd be wrong. This same violation of students' First Amendment rights is present in the halls of even our most prestigious universities. Liberal professors dominate the landscape, and continually put the lie to their claims of tolerance and open-mindedness. Christian student groups are routinely prevented from organizing, their announcements are banned from "free speech zones," and their meetings are denounced as intolerant and either disbanded or they are required to be more inclusive, even if that means violating their religious beliefs and changing the intended purpose of the group. If freedom FROM religion is their goal — and it is — they are succeeding on a grand scale in our schools.

So, where has all of this separation of church and state gotten us? Has it gotten us a more inclusive school system? Has it produced more tolerant children? Absolutely not! It has produced a generation of hate-filled, morally bankrupt adults who haven't the first clue what freedom is. God has been kicked out of our country via the education system, and we are now paying the price. Our public schools have given us the "me" generation. These are individuals who have never read a Bible, and they have no concept of good and evil. If it feels good, it is good, and anyone who disagrees should be sued into silence, or banned from the public arena. They've never lived under Communism, and they've probably never read about it either. They are humanists first and Americans last, and they are taking America down the toilet.

Moral Relativism, the culture of death, divorce, and meaningless spirituality threatens to bring a great superpower to its knees. This will be the topic of the next chapter. America is at yet another tipping point and the question is, will America survive the moral relativism that says it's an act of love to starve a young woman to death when she becomes an inconvenience, or to murder a healthy baby just days before its birth? Read on.

Note: *Please also be sure to read Appendix 1 on Religious Freedom and Public Schools.*

CHAPTER FOUR

MORAL RELATIVISM,
SITUATION ETHICS,
By Any Name, It Was
THE BEGINNING OF SOCIAL ROT

"The Struggle for the Soul of America"

> *The wide acceptance of relativism*
> *has rendered Europe, [for instance],*
> *weak, confused, and chaotic.*
>
> **Bill O'Reilly in**
> *Culture Warrior*

The gaping hole left in the fabric of our society when our Christian heritage and foundation was abandoned was, unfortunately, filled with a humanist view of moral relativism. Call it that or situation ethics, by any name it was the beginning of social rot, the struggle for the soul of America.

Moral relativists invaded that spiritual vacuum with their self-serving belief that ethical standards, morality, and positions of right or wrong are subject to the cultural views and personal choice of each individual. In other words, what is right for one person might not be right for another, and what is immoral or unethical for one person, might be seen as morally acceptable and perfectly ethical to another. The goal was to eliminate moral absolutes, and excuse behavior, no matter how horrific, offensive, or harmful, based solely on the perception of the person engaging in the behavior. This godless worldview has brought us to a tipping point on the edge of societal collapse in America, and ushered in an era of moral, political, and financial crisis. The abhorrent theology of moral relativism has given us the corporate, political, and personal greed that threatens to topple our financial institutions.

"SITUATION ETHICS"

In the 1960s the American Ethics professor and Episcopal Priest Joseph Fletcher trumpeted a new ethic for the world in his book *Situation Ethics*. Fletcher undercut any moral absolutes in human ethics by suggesting that absolutes should only be applied to the best of one's ability for each given situation, thus freeing individuals from living under any absolute moral law, such as those truths found in the Christian Bible. Fletcher blandly suggested that the only absolute that is universally good is love. Therefore, individuals should do whatever love dictates in any given situation. Without an absolute definition of what love is, as is given to us in the Bible, the loving thing to do is always what feels best to the one doing it.

Fletcher expounded in his book, "The situationist enters into every decision-making situation fully armed with the ethical maxims of his community and his heritage, and he treats them with respect as illuminators of his problems. Just the same, he is prepared in any situation to compromise them or set them aside in the situation, if love seems better served by doing so."[1] God's laws, the Bible's moral code, and any moral absolutes our Creator expected us to follow can be tossed aside any time it feels more loving to do so. It does not take an Einstein to figure out what libidinous college students, high on drugs at a frat party, would discern "love" telling them to do. If the 1960s university student was a cultural bomb waiting to go off, Fletcher's book helped light the fuse.

Fletcher may have fired the first shot, but many a philosopher has aimed the same gun at the moral absolutes of the Ten Commandments and the Word of God. More recently, the heretical former Episcopal Bishop of Newark, New Jersey, John Shelby Spong turned the moral law of God upside down, deriding the very absolutes that he swore to protect when the Episcopal Church made him a bishop and overseer of the Christian faith. Spong's impact on society as a theologian was imparted through his writings, his time as rector of several churches, and his prominent lectures at major American theological institutions, including Yale and Harvard Divinity School.

Spong's spurious teachings filled young Christian minds in America and Europe with a "modern" version of Christianity that denied Christ's deity, the virgin birth, and the resurrection. His writings chastised the popular, literal translation of the Bible as outdated and not in line with a contemporary understanding of the universe. He preferred a more nuanced approach to the Scriptures that allowed for a more modern conception of God's nature, and a less restrictive view of good and evil. This assault on the moral absolutes and truths of the Bible was carried to an extreme with Spong. He believed the Bible to be pre-Darwinian mythology, and considered the idea that God intervenes in the lives of men through miracles to be pre-Newtonian nonsense. It's not surprising then, that Spong supported gay marriage, was pro-abortion, condoned premarital sex, and ordained homosexuals to the ministry. In short, Spong threw his support behind every kind of evil imaginable, while devoting his life to the destruction of any, and all, moral absolutes in society. Of the Ten Commandments, he wrote, "There is no external, objective, revealed standard writ in scripture or on tablets of stone that will govern our ethical behavior for all time."[2]

ACADEMIA'S PLACE AT THE TABLE: THE TAKEOVER OF AMERICA'S COLLEGES AND UNIVERSITIES

Moral relativism certainly had its founding fathers in these men, but it is the liberal academic community that is the true locus of moral relativism. The "open-minded" elites that dominate the professorial landscape of American universities live by one rule — never suggest to anyone that anything is absolute. This moral relativism has led to the ridiculous multiculturalism that deems the words of William Shakespeare and John Milton ("dead white men") inferior to the wild ravings of a guru of Eastern Mysticism, or the spiritual illumination of some shaman in an oceanic backwater. Universities now offer courses in Yoga Psychology, Tarot Card Reading, Psychic Development and Techniques, Astrology, Self-Awareness Through Self-Hypnosis, among other equally irrelevant, pseudo-spiritual topics that will prepare them for precisely nothing in the real world.[3]

At America's oldest school of theology, Harvard Divinity School, students sit in the lotus position mindlessly parroting New Age chants, but no longer sing traditional hymns. The school paper, "The Nave", announces on its calendar that March 20th is "a special time to listen to the Buddha and meditate on the perfection of enlightenment", yet there is no mention of Palm Sunday, or Passover.[4]

Schools that were founded to prepare students for the ministry and instill in them knowledge of biblical truths became bastions of secular multiculturalism, and their new mission was to cleanse society of any Christian values. They mastered the Stalinist tactic of forcing a cultural shift on the entire country through indoctrination and the corruption of our children's minds. The swiftly moving danger of what the Obama administration is proposing and doing can be seen in the advice, consent, and backing of the liberal Congress as they, sheep like, follow the agenda of their leader.

Statistics now reveal that as many as two out of three Christian teens will lose their faith by the time they finish college. They are walking away from God; their faith has been undermined and destroyed by what they are finding at even some Christian colleges today. This is very sobering. It prompts the incredulous reaction of why! It calls for serious contemplation, what can we do? How can we turn the tide?

Liberal professors in a state or private university today hold a place of unchallenged authority, and if they have tenure, you cannot blow them out of their ivory tower with any amount of scholastic dynamite. They delight in filling the unformed minds of teenagers with the bilge water of their own moral and spiritual bankruptcy. Alienated from productive society, paid from a large university endowment, the liberal professor is accountable to no one. They are free to spout whatever lunacy they wish in the name of academic freedom. In truth, the only ideas freely exchanged in the American university are the liberal talking points that rain down from the spiraled towers of the Ivy League schools where these professors live in utter separation from the day-to-day world of the working public.

During the formative years of a fledgling American democracy, Harvard, Yale, and Princeton were founded to train gospel ministers, yet they ultimately followed each other into the sinkhole of liberal relativism. The flowers of our nation's youth would henceforth be educated in a godless environment of multiculturalism, far from the moral values of their ancestors. William Buckley wrote his famous *God and Man At Yale* in a protest against the godless liberalism of his own alma mater, an act for which God has surely pardoned him, but not Yale! He indicted one of America's most prestigious universities for abandoning the very principles that were its foundation, undermining the purpose for which it had originated, and denying its students any sense of individualism by forcing them to embrace the burgeoning creed of liberalism. Up to the last moment before his death Buckley and the political force of his book has been a thorn in the side of the liberal establishment. However, the dark tenets of moral relativism remain the foundation of our curriculum and the religion of the majority of our educators to this day. More than ever, the moral relativists are winning the battle for our children's minds.

Will what happened in Europe — where secular culture has replaced the traditional religious landscape — happen here? Or has it already happened because so many traditional Americans are ignoring the escalating culture war? Bill O'Reilly talks about this at length in his book *Culture Warrior.* He discusses how countries like Spain, France, and Italy, once devoutly Catholic, have now moved away from organized religion and are increasingly embracing secular culture. He says "The free fall of tradition is most noticeable in Northern Europe where the percentage of people attending weekly church services is down to the single digits in places like Holland and Scandinavia." O'Reilly, himself a Catholic, decries what has happened, for instance, in Italy, the historic seat of the Catholic Church, where attendance at mass has plummeted as the secular-progressive culture has swept away traditional beliefs. He points out that the wide acceptance of relativism has rendered Europe weak, confused, and chaotic.

I applaud O'Reilly for his concern and stance. He rightly asks "So which side are you on in the culture war? Or are you sitting things out?"

He calls this "the struggle for the soul of America." Strong stuff! He himself applauds the conservative Christian groups that are most engaged on the traditional side, but he doesn't believe this culture war will be won in the religious arena. "Even though the Christian groups are effective in getting their traditional message out, they are outgunned."

But wait, Mr. O'Reilly, Christians have an unseen, but powerful force on our side, and you will remember from biblical accounts, as well as God's intervention in the affairs of men and nations through history, how, in response to prayer and the efforts of God's people, He has come through for us. Yes, now is the time to rally the troops, as they say, but even more importantly for us, as Christians, to cry out to God and His army of unseen hosts, to do battle for us. That's where our strength and power comes from, and God is always on the side of the right. I could point to account after account in the Bible where this is vividly portrayed, but suffice right here to ask readers to open up the Word of God and mine its depths and discover for themselves what God does for His people.

But in case you are unconvinced about the inroads being made by the moral relativists, what follows is comparatively recent history; this is indisputable factually, and convincingly correct.

WILLIAM AYERS

During the 2008 Presidential election, some of us learned about another one of these professors who kindly spends tax dollars to indoctrinate our children, just as they are entering adulthood. After denying that he even knew him, and then pretending that he was "just another guy in the neighborhood," President Obama admitted to having a personal, and working relationship with the domestic terrorist, and founder of the Weather Underground, Bill Ayers. Ayers and his gang of admitted Communists and Marxists are responsible for bombing the Pentagon, the Capital Building, and several other government buildings during the height of the 1960s antiwar movement. Obama distanced himself from Ayers' terrorism, arguing that the actual bombings took place when he was only eight years old. He conveniently avoided discussion of Ayers own admission, made as recently as 2002, that he only wished he could have done more damage. It's not as if Ayers had been rehabilitated when Obama knew, and worked with him on the Annenberg foundation's Board of Directors, and held campaign fund raisers at Ayers' house.

Obama further excused the relationship by telling Americans that Ayers was a "respected educator," and Professor of English at Columbia University. I'm sure many were persuaded by this defense of Ayers' character, and media attention given to the Obama/Ayers association was likely dismissed by many as the ravings of the "vast Right Wing conspiracy." After all, a respected university had seen fit to give Ayers tenure, and his books are standard fare among educators and university elites across the country. As it turns out, Ayers employment at Columbia University was probably more a result of his wealthy father's vast connections in Chicago, than his qualifications as an educator. It was, nevertheless, used to discredit any criticism of his years as a fugitive.

Americans are, unfortunately too quick to assume that being a university professor is a positive testament to one's character. Universities in Florida have employed professors who were later arrested for funding terrorism, and actively supporting terrorist Jihad[5]. Columbia University has a long list of openly Communist and Marxist Professors who have been filling young minds with their theology of "social justice," "critical pedagogy," and such nonsense as "queer theory" for years[6]. A professorship at an American university, unfortunately, is not an automatic, ringing endorsement of one's moral stature, or conduct as a human being.

If you hadn't heard of William Ayers, or the Weather Underground before reading this book, it wouldn't be surprising. During the last election, the mainstream media specialized in covering up anything that might negatively impact the campaign of Barrack Obama. Past associations, his days as president of the Harvard Law Review, his years at Columbia, where he was first drawn to Marxist ideology, and the twenty years he spent listening to the racist Liberation Theology of Pastor Jeremiah Wright were ignored, dismissed, or excused using the same moral relativism the media used to excuse corruption and deceit during the Clinton years.

Ayers' history and connection to Obama should have been on the front page of every newspaper in the country for weeks. It was as damning as any scandal to plague a presidential candidates run for office in history. We are, after all, living in a time of declared war on the very terrorist mentality that led Ayers to wage Marxist Jihad on his own country.

William Ayers wasn't just a terrorist; he was a founding member of the Weather Underground, an antiwar organization formed in 1969 in response to the Vietnam War. The group's stated intent was to overthrow the U.S. government by any means necessary. The Weather Underground's first manifesto stated, "The main struggle going on in the world today is between U.S. imperialism and the national liberation struggles against it." The group's "white fighting force," as they called themselves, went on a rampage through America engaging in street fighting, riots, beatings, pipe bombings, and attacks on the police, all culminating in the infamous Days of Rage in Chicago.[7] Following the formation of a so-called "National War Council," they took the group underground and began a bombing campaign that would target several government buildings, and even Fort Dix. The media repeated over and over that the Underground had injured no one in their campaign of terror, but the victims of their attacks would probably beg to differ. Joseph Skelly reported the following in his article, "Unearthing the Weather Underground:"

> *In February 1970 the Weather Underground firebombed the home of John Murtagh, a New York City judge, with his entire family barely escaping the conflagration. On March 6 a massive nail bomb intended to kill and maim soldiers at Fort Dix, NJ prematurely detonated in a townhouse in Greenwich Village, killing three members, Ted Gold, Diana Oughton, and Terry Robbins, while two others, Katy Boudin and Cathy Wilkerson, managed to elude capture. "Operating under the logic that 'the bigger the bang the better,'" Dan Berger notes, "the action was to be a pre-emptive strike against those who would soon drop bombs over Vietnam, thus 'bringing the war home' with all the intensity the slogan implied."[8]*

Murtagh's son, who was nine at the time, recounted what he experienced the night the Weather Underground threw bombs at his family home, and placed a car bomb under the family car. Read the following, and see if you agree with the media's verdict that no one had been harmed by what Ayers did, and they never intended to injure or kill anyone.

> *I still recall, as though it were a dream, thinking that someone was lifting and dropping my bed as the explosions jolted me awake, and I remember my mother's pulling me from the tangle of sheets and running to the kitchen where my father stood. Through the large windows overlooking the yard, all we could see was the bright glow of flames below. We didn't leave our burning house for fear of who might be waiting outside. The same night, bombs were thrown at a police car in Manhattan and two military recruiting stations in Brooklyn. Sunlight, the next morning revealed three sentences of blood-red graffiti on our sidewalk: FREE THE PANTHER 21; THE VIET CONG HAVE WON; KILL THE PIGS.*
>
> *Though no one was ever caught or tried for the attempt on my family's life, there was never any doubt who was behind it. Only a few weeks after the attack, the New York contingent of the Weathermen blew themselves up making more bombs in a Greenwich Village townhouse. The same cell had bombed my house, writes Ron Jacobs in* The Way the Wind Blew: A History of the Weather Underground. *And in late November that year, a letter to the Associated Press signed by Bernardine Dohrn, Ayers's wife, promised more bombings.*[9]

Neither the media, nor Barack Obama, or even Bill Ayers himself can convince me that they did not intend to kill or injure someone that night. If we must give Ayers credit for being intelligent enough to be a university professor, then we must also be willing to admit that he is intelligent enough to know that throwing bombs at a house from two sides, and planting a bomb under a car filled with fuel in the driveway, while the family is sleeping inside, is likely to result in the family being killed in the ensuing house fire. The only thing that saved the Murtagh family was probably the alert neighbor who managed to put out the fire started under their car before it could reach the fuel tank and explode. They intentionally put an innocent man and his family in grave danger, terrorized his children, and left them wondering when the attackers might be back to make good on their threatening message. No, Bill Ayers never harmed anyone! It was just a little peaceful, civil disobedience. The truth is, Bill Ayers and his ilk were, and are, nothing more than attempted murderers, thugs, and terrorists. It's telling that the American media would claim no one was hurt in their bombings, and never mention what happened to the Murtagh family, or that three of their own died when a bomb meant for soldiers at Fort Briggs went off a bit sooner than expected. It's equally tragic that millions of American's believed them, and elected someone to be their president who supped with, worked with, and befriended a man like William Ayers.

It is Ayers' "contribution" to the academic world, however, that stands to do the greatest damage to our nation, through his own courses and his contribution to the education system as a whole. Ayers admits to being a "communist street fighter," and student of Karl Marx and Malcolm X. He speaks openly of his mission to turn America's schools into indoctrination centers where children will become revolutionaries, steeped in the philosophy of wealth redistribution, and eager to promote the State as the only way to achieve "social justice" for everyone. His course titled "On Urban Education" is dripping with the same Socialist bile spewed forth by the Stalinists of Communist Russia, and repeated most recently by Barack Obama in response to a question asked by "Joe the Plumber." Obama demonstrated his agreement with his friend, Professor Ayers, when he told Joe "things work better when you spread the wealth around." Joe wanted to keep his hard-earned tax dollars to start the plumbing business he'd always wanted, but the Columbia-taught Obama had learned long ago that equality must come through government control of the wealth, to be distributed as he sees fit. Joe just needed to understand that his American Dream must be sacrificed for the good of the many.

One would think that professors like Ayers would be ostracized, making up only a fringe group of radical educators in Academia that are tolerated, but not promoted. But, that couldn't be further from reality. In fact, his peers recently elected him Vice President for Curriculum of the American Education Research Association (AERA), which is the largest organization of education school professors and researchers in the country![10]

So, what kind of educational excellence will you find in one of Professor Ayers' classes that is so worthy of the AERA's admiration? You will find courses with such required reading as Brazilian, Marxist Paolo Freire's "Pedagogy of the Oppressed," a book by radical feminist and critical race theorist, Bell Hooks; two of Ayers own books; and a "Freedom School Curriculum." In other words, students will discuss, read, hear lectures on, and debate Marxist Socialism, Marxist Socialism, and more Marxist Socialism, with a hint of the race card thrown in for those future liberal politicians in the class.

One particular class taught by Bill Ayers called, "Social Conflicts of the 1960s," promotes the Liberation Theology of his days as a Weatherman, and advocates that schools be used to promote revolutionary fervor among the "oppressed" in society. The oppressed, of course, are all those who agree that the government is both the **source** of their problems and lack of success, and the **answer** to all of their problems, by way of taxation and wealth redistribution. This is, by the way, the same social theology preached every Sunday by Jeremiah Wright from the pulpit of Barrack Obama's former church. It's not hard to see where Obama picked up his affinity for Socialist politics. He learned it in the same institutions of "higher" learning where his younger supporters were denied an education on the dangers of Socialism, and its complete and utter failure throughout history.

These are the "educators" we trust to prepare our children for employment, to produce our future leaders, and, in some cases, preach in our churches. Is it any wonder we continue to elect dishonest, big spending, corrupt politicians to govern us? A growing segment of our population has been taught to trust change for the sake of change, as long as corporations and people of faith are blamed for every social ill, while productive, successful people are made to foot the bill as penance.

DUMBING DOWN OUR CHILDREN

A godless aversion to any absolute standard of behavior and morals is not a worldview held only by those who have been successfully indoctrinated by university professors. From the moment our children enter their very first kindergarten classroom, the process of dumbing them down, and re-educating them into the religion of liberal tolerance and cultural sensitivity begins. Students reach the university fully versed in the terminology and ideology necessary for instantly assuaging all guilt, shrugging off any accountability for life choices, and redefining, either culturally or spiritually, any moral dilemma that stands in the way of justifying their chosen "path."

The doctrines of moral relativism taught in our schools beginning in elementary school, find anchor first in evolution. Moral relativism requires one to believe that life is without meaning or purpose. It is the result of a random accident, and leads only to death, where each life simply ceases to exist. When there is no life beyond death, then we need not concern ourselves with any rules, restrictions, or consequences for our actions and behavior. Everything is acceptable, the moral relativist reasons, because it ultimately doesn't matter. Why live by a moral code, if there is no consequence for our actions.

This is why moral relativists will so vehemently defend the theory of evolution. Without their faith in Darwin's theory that we are merely highly evolved apes, the only other explanation for the origins of man is some form of intelligent design. If we weren't an accident, we must have been created, and if we were created, we must be subject to the laws and purposes of that Creator. William McGuffey, the author of the McGuffey's Readers used in all of America's public schools from 1836 to the 1920s knew exactly what would happen to a society should its people choose to deny God and live only for themselves. He wrote, "Erase all thought and fear of God from a community, and selfishness and sensuality would absorb the whole man." [11]

Our educators today, whether a university professor, or an elementary school teacher, are teaching our children that there is no such thing as right and wrong. Students hear a version of morality that the Word of God clearly warns us against in Isaiah 5:20, which reads, "Woe to those who call evil good and good evil, who put darkness for light and light for darkness, who put bitter for sweet and sweet for bitter." In contraposition to this verse, our children learn to see good and evil as relative to their own situation, experiences, beliefs, or preferences. It's a spoiled, selfish view of the world that imposes their beliefs on others, and forces those around them to accept excuses, intentions, feelings, and personal beliefs as an excuse for bad behavior. In short, students learn to see the world not as it really is, but how they want it to be.

THE CONCEPT OF "CULTURAL RELATIVISM"

Like so many shifts in modern thought, moral relativism has taken root and spread through our society's core values like the tentacles of the most invasive of noxious weeds. Expanding on these evil doctrines, our educators teach our children that right and wrong can be interpreted differently by different cultures. This concept of cultural relativism promotes the belief that what are good, or evil changes, depend on the perspective of the culture, or the beliefs of the people in that culture. Such a view eschews the idea of any universal right or wrong, effectively destroying any objective standards society might have had, and replacing it with pluralism and tolerance.

With this diminishing list of acceptable standards available to our nation's leaders, legislators are having a more difficult time defining the laws they pass, and our court system is becoming progressively corrupt as societal pressures distort the interpretation of those laws. As a result, laws that govern morality in our society have been deemed intolerant, and lewdness and indecency in our movies, television, and media have reached levels our ancestors never would have imagined they could. Those who don't buy into the reinterpretation of Scripture as put forth by the liberal churches who try to make Christianity palatable to sexual deviants and humanists, are chastised for being intolerant of the cultural beliefs of others, as if disagreeing with someone's spiritual beliefs is tantamount to uttering a racial slur. Cultural relativism's first commandment is that we have no right to judge or punish anyone for anything. We must accept all lifestyles, or be deemed intolerant hate-mongers.

Many Christians have cowered, felt embarrassed about their faith, and given in to this kind of intimidation and name calling. They haven't been given a secure grounding in the Bible, and they don't know how to defend their faith on a logical, scientific, historical, or any other level. In fact they don't even know that they can. They've heard for so long that science and spirituality are incompatible, and they've bought into the lie that Darwin's flawed theory of man's evolution is a proven fact. The number is dwindling of churches and pastors who are willing to counter the theory of evolution and preach to their congregations about the scientific evidence for the existence of a divine Creator. But there are too many who are easily intimidated into accepting that their beliefs can only be supported by faith, and are afraid to defend their position.

UNEQUIPPED CHRISTIANS AND THE DANGER OF CHRISTIANITY'S DWINDLING INFLUENCE

Faith is the basis of our salvation, but God never intended for us to check our brains at the chapel door. He created the wonders and miracles of our complex solar system, and a world so precisely and amazingly designed to support life so that no one could behold its magnificence and doubt the power and existence of God. Evidence of His hand in our existence on this planet abound, and there are many scientists, Ph.D.'s and, yes, even professors who can defend creationism with greater evidentiary support than any honest evolutionist could come up with to defend Darwin. Indeed, it takes far more faith to be an atheist, yet Christians are too often left unarmed and unable to provide an answer when their peers and teachers dismiss the Bible out of hand and argue that religion and science are mutually exclusive. Unequipped Christians feel powerless to throw off the condescending labels and ridicule, and defend the Truth. As a result of Christianity's dwindling influence, and unwillingness to make their case heard, we now live in a country where the vast majority of the population calls themselves Christian, yet our society looks more like a modern-day Sodom and Gomorrah.

This intimidation can begin at an early age. Chuck Colson tells the account of what happened to Becca, a twelve-year-old, who came home from school and a piece of paper dropped out of her notebook. When Amy, her mother, picked it up for her, she saw it was a test on the topic, "How did the universe come into existence?"

Becca had given the answer the teacher expected, which was at odds with what Becca had been learning at home and at church.

"Why'd you put that, honey?" Amy asked. "You know that we believe that God created the universe. It didn't just come to be out of nothing."

Becca buirst into tears. "I know, Mom, "she said. "But if I had answered that way I would have failed the test."

Now this story has a happy ending, but not all such accounts do, and many could be cited. But Amy made an appointment to see the teacher. In a nonconfrontive way Amy explained, from a scientific perspective, what their family believed and laid out the evidence of why they believed it. The teacher said she needed to talk to the principal.

Not intimidated, Amy made an appointment to see the principal and laid out her case again. The principal listened carefully and then called in the teacher. "You need to teach the kids that the origins of the universe as you are teaching them are in fact a theory, and not meant to contradict anything they're learning at home. I think you need to apologize to them."

The upshot of that was that the teacher agreed to do so; then the principal asked the mother to serve on the school's curriculum committee. Amy was able to bring a biblically informed world-view influence to that public school. Any of us can do the same. This is a great story and should encourage any parent to be bold, in this way, and trust God to help us in what we may be timid about doing.

With the new societal laws of behavior dictating that we never judge, criticize, or even disagree with someone's moral convictions, abhorrent behavior has become quite simple to defend. Because behavior deemed offensive by some can be justified by the moral depravity of the majority, the "everybody's doing it" defense becomes an acceptable adult argument. Grown men and women, legislators, governors, and media reporters stand before society and shout "but they do it too!!"

From time to time, I tortured myself by watching Hannity and Colmes on Fox News. As the program airs now, Alan Colmes is no longer on the show, but during the coverage of the 2008 presidential election, he was. We saw how Hannity's liberal counterpart made an art form out of using moral relativism to argue his point of view. During the coverage of the election, the left-wing blogs and the liberal media launched the most despicable smear campaign in political history against McCain's Vice Presidential pick, Sarah Palin.

The children of politicians have traditionally been sheltered from the media's attack-dog tactics, as it has been rightly reasoned they are not running for office, and should not be drug through the mud with their parents. The nomination of a pro-life, conservative woman, however, was more than the liberal media and Barack Obama supporters could stand. Conspiracy theories demonizing this little-known, but extremely popular, governor of Alaska saturated the news for days. Palin was accused of hiding her daughter's pregnancy by claiming the baby was hers. Her daughter, who had become pregnant out of wedlock, was relentlessly attacked for her mistake, and both she and her mother, who had given birth recently to a baby with Down syndrome, were criticized for not aborting the "unwanted" babies. Palin had lived her beliefs by giving birth to a baby that she knew would have Down Syndrome, prompting Alan Colmes to pontificate that Palin probably didn't get the proper pre-natal care, and shouldn't have had the child, since babies born to mothers in their forties are more likely to have birth defects such as Down's Syndrome. A woman's right to choose, according to the liberals, ends when they choose to have their baby, rather than kill it.

JUSTIFYING THE UNJUSTIFIABLE

When Colmes was called out for his vicious attack on Sarah Palin's choice to have a child with a birth defect, he did as he always does, and whined that Republicans do it, too. Pointing to the "Swift Boat Vets for Truth" advertisements that put the final nail in the coffin of John Kerry's presidential campaign in 2002, he excused the alleged abuse of his media pulpit by pointing to the actions of others. Alan had long complained about what he sees as unfair smear tactics used by Republicans, yet he used the very behavior he once denounced to defend his own actions. This is the irrational logic of the moral relativist. It's wrong for you to do it, and I have a right to judge you for it, but I also have the right to justify doing the same thing because you did it first. Like a child who got caught stealing their sister's toy, they point fingers, act indignant, and tell their critics it's not fair to judge them. They can't see their own hypocrisy, and it doesn't occur to them that a despicable act becomes no less despicable by pointing to the same despicable act done by someone else. And so, cultural relativism justifies the unjustifiable, and makes it the new norm.

This process of cultural devolution through excuses has brought us pornography, rising divorce rates, debauchery on our streets and in our homes, and the slaughter of countless unwanted babies. What would have shocked previous generations isn't even noticed in today's society. Pornographic ads grace the sides of buses and trains in our cities, and movies are frequently rated R for "extreme religious content", while movies filled with nudity, sex, and filth are rated PG-13.

I know some of you might think that the Hollywood movie rating system is sufficient to guide parents and children as to what movies they should be watching. If you have placed your trust in this system, consider the following descriptions from reviews written by Vice & Hicks, professional movie critics, of PG-13 rated movies.

28 DAYS	PG-13 for "profanity, sex, substance abuse"
AIRHEADS	PG-13 for "considerable raunchiness; there is violence, graphic sex, profanity and vulgarity"
BIG KAHUNA	R for "frequent use of strong profanity and crude slang, some off-color discussions"
BIRD ON A WIRE	PG-13 for "considerable mayhem, as well as sex, profanity and some nudity"

BLAME IT ON THE BELLBOY	PG-13 for "sadistic, graphic violence, as well as sex, profanity, vulgarity, and some partial nudity"
BOWFINGER	PG-13 for "violence, gore, profanity, vulgarity, racial epithets"
BROKEDOWN PALACE	PG-13 for "profanity, a violent beating, simulated drug use (marijuana), use of crude slang terms and vulgar gestures, and brief female nudity"

These movies, available to thirteen-year-old children with the guidance of misguided parents, contain language and situations that would not have been tolerated in a saloon in earlier generations. We must remember that *profanity is progressive.* What shocks one generation does not even phase the next generation. I tremble to think what the next generation will hear and say in the public assemblies of our schools, cities, and recreational centers. Our public and private language will be such a moral gutter and verbal rottenness that the very air around us will stink with the noxious smell of hell itself. No wonder the terrorists of Islam target our culture as one of moral rot. As misguided as these sons of Allah may be, the profanity and taking of the name of God in vain that they detest, characterizes our nation at every level of social culture.

THE DECLINE OF THE FAMILY

As new generations of our children are indoctrinated, then sent out by our universities into a world steeped in the ways of political correctness, they are equipped to do little more than play the role of a victim. They demand that government provide the American dream FOR them, and their lack of any moral compass or conscience becomes even more evident in their marriages, parenting skills, and their children.

If anyone doubts that the attitude toward the American family has changed, they need only compare the first full-term president of the twentieth century with the last — Theodore Roosevelt in contrast to William Jefferson Clinton. Theodore Roosevelt became president following the assassination of William McKinley in 1901. He served out the latter's term and was then re-elected by the widest margin in history. During Roosevelt's presidency the nation witnessed the charming family life of a husband and gentleman, his devoted wife Edith Kermit Roosevelt, and their six children. TR's favorite pastime was to row his wife Edith across Oyster Bay. His tender letters to her and to his six children resound with love and Christian fatherhood. He was a Christian, a churchman, and a devout friend of the clergy. His famous biographer Edmund Morris pays the highest compliment that might be paid to such a public figure. Morris writes that the Roosevelts were the very incarnation of the marriage vow for the entire nation.[12] Living under the white heat of political inspection, surrounded by many enemies, Roosevelt never once was accused of anything other than fidelity to his marriage and family. In fact, Henry Adams once had to remind TR that the President only believed the Ten Commandments, he did not write them.

Fast forward to the end of the twentieth century, and to the occupant of the White House during the nineties, William Jefferson Clinton. He came to the presidency surrounded by rumors of an extramarital affair with a nightclub torch singer[13], and amidst accusations that he had sexually harassed an Arkansas state employee while he was governor of that state.[14] Finally, he lied to the entire world about the nature of his relationship with a White House intern, and, after a protracted battle with the media and special prosecutors assigned to investigate grounds for impeachment, he shamefully confessed before the nation that he had abused the most power-ful office in the world to have a sexual encounter with a girl young enough to be his daughter. He lied to his wife, his daughter, and the world.

In TR's day a President would have been impeached immediately for such conduct. In Clinton's era, much of the nation supported him, and his party labeled the ensuing impeachment hearings as nothing more than a political witch-hunt, as if such abhorrent behavior, and the perjury that was punished by the Bar Association with the revocation of his license to practice law, was nothing but a private matter. Is it any wonder that the American family has changed? The support given to one of the most popular First Families in recent history proves that it has, and certainly not for the better.

Statistics support what the change in the White House demonstrates. The United States has the highest divorce rate in the entire world. Out of every thousand marriages in this country, 500 of them will end in divorce. That means nearly half of all newlyweds in the United Stated end up divorced, and the divorce rate for second marriages is even higher than that. [15]

EFFECTS OF DIVORCE

All studies demonstrate that divorce has a profound and lifelong impact on children. A twenty-year-study of children whose parents were divorced in the seventies demonstrates the impact of divorce follows children into their adult lives with expectations of failure, fear of loss, fear of change, and fear of conflict.[16] (Please allow me to remind the reader this is not condemnation upon those who have experienced this pain and loss. Divorce is not the unpardonable sin and the grace and mercy of Christ provides life beyond divorce. That said, I do not want to fail to remind all of us of the consequences of this scourge upon society and just perhaps, someone will read this and rethink their pending decision.)

Divorce is expensive for the government, leads to juvenile offenders, early sexual experimentation, and disrupts children's development. Consider the following facts from scientific studies on the long-term effects of divorce on children. Children living with both biological parents are 20 to 35 percent more physically healthy than children from broken homes. ("Marriage, Divorce and Children's Adjustment", Robert E. Emery, Sage Publications, 1988). Perhaps our politicians who are concerned about children and families without healthcare should examine the effect of divorce on those statistics, and admit that family values are in fact important to our culture.

Another study, *The Long Term Impact of Divorce on Children: A First Report from a 25-Year Study*, written by Judith Wallerstein, and published in 1991 by the Journal of the American Academy of Child and Adolescent Psychiatry, concluded that children, even six years after a parental marriage breakup, tended to be lonely, unhappy, anxious and insecure.[17] Children of divorce are also four times more likely to report problems with peers and friends than children whose parents have kept their marriages intact.[18]   Other studies reveal that 70 percent of long-term prison inmates grew up in broken homes. Children of divorce are also at a greater risk of experiencing injury, asthma, headaches, and speech defects than children of married parents, and people who come from broken families are almost twice as likely to attempt suicide than those who do not come from broken homes.[19] America is at a tipping point in the education and up-bringing of our children, and the absence of family values in our culture is sending our children over a cliff into a morass of moral depravity and a life of fear and insecurity.

Added to the disastrous divorce rate in this country, are the statistics of the last Census concerning the soaring increase of illegitimate births. In one decade, 1980 to 1992, the single parent birth rate rose by 54 percent in the U.S., the largest increase ever recorded.[20] Consider this sobering fact. In 1950 the illegitimacy rate was about 4 percent and only 5.3 percent in 1960. While some consider this to be a minority problem, in reality it is a growing problem among people of all ethnicities and income levels. Today, nearly 30 percent of all births are illegitimate. Among blacks, the illegitimacy rate is nearly two-thirds of all births, and among whites, it tops 22 percent.[21] This is not just a minority problem, but a growing cultural problem. Interestingly, there is strong evidence to support the availability of welfare as being connected to the increase in out-of-wedlock births. With government handouts guaranteed to unwed mothers, increasing in amount with the birth of each illegitimate child, babies have become a source of income, rather than a treasured new member of the family.[22]

Go to any big city hospital, look at the nursery with the babies lined up in orderly rows, and count them. Let the staggering statistic sink in that one out of four of those babies was conceived and born out of wedlock. They were born in a home that knows nothing about marriage, and they will in all statistical probability grow up to produce the same kind of family, with their children facing the same cultural difficulties that they did.

The words "family values" have been turned into the equivalent of political curse words by the media and politicians on the Left. They win elections by labeling people of faith the "far right", and casting them as a fringe group bent on cramming their religion down people's throats. Their constituents remain blissfully unaware of the consequences that will affect every one of us, if our children continue to grow up in broken homes.

THE DEVALUATION OF THE INSTITUTION OF MARRIAGE

Chicago is the broad-shouldered city of Midwestern values. Most do not consider Chicago to suffer from the secularism of New York City or the hedonism of Hollywood. Chicago is the breadbasket and the butcher of America, filled with the descendants of stolid immigrants who built a mighty city out of the prairie. Yet, in Chicago's inner city neighborhoods, only one in ten babies are born to married parents.[23] There is not a single bridal shop on Chicago's West Side. As an institution, marriage has virtually disappeared from an entire section of this great Midwestern city. Marriage has become the remote goal of a few of the people who cohabit. Rather than being a beginning point from which life is worked out, couples who produce half a dozen children out of wedlock imagine the day when they might get married. Marriage for these people is not a commitment from which life is built, but a distant goal imagined in a better future.

Consider Oklahoma. Most think of Oklahoma as the repository of staunch American values. When we think of the characters in the great musical *Oklahoma*, we imagine farms, and families, and faith. Yet, in 1990 Oklahoma had the second highest divorce rate in America, and in 2005 it had improved only slightly to the fourth highest.[24] The problem was so severe in the nineties that, in June of 1999, Governor Frank Keating took action by convening the *Governor's and First Lady's Conference on Marriage*, bringing together leaders from the business community, religious congregations, education, and government, as well as service providers and the media, to forge the nation's first state action plan for reducing divorce.

In March 2000, Keating announced a $10 million marriage initiative, earmarking 10 percent of the state's surplus funds to encourage people to think more carefully before making the decision to marry.[25]

President Bush also dedicated time during his presidency to promote a growing marriage movement that recognizes the enormous social consequences of divorce and the disintegration of homes. These efforts are commendable, yet the divorce rate continues to grow on a national level.

Long-term studies have clearly indicated the impact of divorce on teenage children. While it was once thought that divorce primarily hurt younger children, the results of long-term studies demonstrate that the harsher impact of divorce is on teenagers. In parental divorce, boys were seen to suffer more drug addiction than girls. The other bad news, however, is that girls were more likely to suffer from drug abuse if their parents remarried. Either way, the scene is bad and the news is discouraging.

Furthermore, marital instability transmits itself across generational lines. A study by Paul R. Amato and Danelle D. Deboer in *Journal of Marriage and Family* 63 (November 2001) demonstrates from detailed research that children of divorce are touched by the intergenerational impact of divorce in two substantial ways. First, they learn from what they see, and they will adopt their parent's impaired communication skills. Couples who divorce teach their children negative emotions, criticism of their partners, defensiveness, withdrawal from problem-solving, difficulty resolving conflict, unwillingness to spend time with one another, and more problems with jealousy, infidelity, moodiness, and controlling anger. Research demonstrates that the children of divorce learn these behaviors from their divorced parents, and duplicate them in their own lives. Marriage partners with divorced parents demonstrate more communication problems than those with parents who remained in marriages, even when the marriages were only marginal.

As adults, children of divorce demonstrate interpersonal styles that appear to impact the quality of their own marriages negatively. That is to say, children learn dysfunctional marital behavior by observing it. That is not the only bad news, however, from this research. When children observe a lack of commitment, they are more likely to duplicate that lack of commitment in their own lives. When children watch their parents divorce, they learn up close that marriage does not last for a lifetime, that people do not have to stay in relationships, and that divorce can offer the opportunity for a new partner. Parents with a strong commitment to marriage demonstrate to their children that problems should be solved and their children, in turn, take the longer-term perspective that relationships can be renewed and restored.

Moral relativism has taken a horrible toll on so many areas of our culture, leaving us with broken homes, children with little or no direction, an education system that promotes mediocrity, and a population that cannot identify evil in their own lives, in society, or in those they elect to lead them. In the next chapter, we'll look in more detail at what moral relativism has done to our society, the greed that has taken root, and the price we are now paying for losing our national conscience. Protecting ourselves from any judgment or criticism, and turning our backs on the biblical moral code our nation was founded on has done much damage. As you will read, America has reached a tipping point in history, and a return to the values and beliefs of those great Christians who founded this country is imperative, if we are to survive as a nation.

CHAPTER FIVE

GREED AT EVERY LEVEL
In the Grip of Greed

The god of greed is a cheat.

John White in *The Golden Cow*
Materialism in the Twentieth-
[and Twenty-First-] Century Church

M oral relativism, the indoctrination of several generations of children by Socialist atheists, and the abundance of liberal lobbying groups who have corrupted our education system, have led to a dog eat dog world where class warfare, government pandering, and every color and stripe of greed dominates our nation. It seems a majority of Americans no longer have regard for the Bible's command to help others who are in need, and they spend far more time pointing fingers at whatever political group or economic class of people they believe are responsible for their failures in life, than they do working for the American dream.

This is not to say that America isn't a generous nation. While the rest of the world, those afflicted by the same greed and envy, rarely gives us credit for it, we are still the most generous nation on Earth. Americans give hundreds of billions of dollars to countries desperate for help, and to charitable causes, and those amounts rise each year at a rate faster than the U.S. economy as a whole. Even in bad economic times, Americans dig deep and keep giving to those less fortunate than themselves. No other developed country even approaches the level of American charitable giving. For example, in 1995, Americans gave three and a half times as much to causes and charities as the French, seven times as much as the Germans, and fourteen times as much as the Italians! And, it's not just money Americans give. In 1998, Americans were 15 percent more likely to volunteer their time than the Dutch, 21 percent more likely than the Swiss, and 32 percent more likely than the Germans. Studies also show that these vast differences in a willingness to give are not attributable to education level, income, age, sex, or marital status. No matter the circumstances, Americans are more likely to give money and time to help others than any other group of people on Earth.[1]

So, when I talk about this country's growing problem with greed and self-serving corruption, I'm not speaking of the American people as a whole, but rather segments of our culture, economy, and government that have been corrupted by power, success, and an abandonment of the moral truths America was founded upon. I'm speaking of the CEO's who now reside in federal prisons, corrupt politicians that got caught with their hand in the cookie jar, and government programs that are based more on payback for political favors, lobbying, campaigns contributions, and power hungry egos than on what is best for the country and the American people. With that said, we do still have a growing number of people, Christians included, who think only of their own self interests and what they can get from their government, their neighbors, and their employers, often to the detriment of others.

CORPORATE GREED

Most have probably heard of the Enron Corporation, and their role in setting off the largest wave of accounting scandals, corporate corruption, and insider trading scandals in history. Enron's collapse currently stands as the largest single act of fraud in American history. As of this writing, most of the major players and executives in the Enron scandal have been convicted of numerous felonies, including securities and wire fraud, bank fraud, money laundering, insider trading, and other financial crimes. Several of these executives are now serving time in federal prisons, with the exception of the Chairman of the Board, Kenneth Lay, who died of a heart attack while awaiting sentencing.

The Enron Corporation, in its prime, was the seventh largest company in America with revenue exceeding $100 billion, and over 20,000 employees. In the early 1990s, under the Clinton Administration, the Congress of the United States of America passed legislation deregulating the sale of electricity. This made it possible for companies like Enron to thrive, but also caused price volatility in the market, much to the aggravation of energy producers and several state governments. However, because of strong political lobbying by Enron, and large campaign contributions given to the right people, the flawed system was kept in place.

While Enron was paying off politicians to keep the Enron-friendly legislation coming, they were also creating offshore entities to be used for avoiding taxes, and for hiding the huge losses the company was taking off their balance sheets. As a result, Enron looked like it was making billions in profits, while it was actually losing money. This in turn drove up the stock price, and executives began to work on insider information to trade millions of dollars in Enron stock. The investors knew nothing of these offshore accounts, or the losses Enron was hiding to make themselves appear profitable.

Following the deregulation that allowed Enron to expand its empire, Enron gave money to politicians' hand-over-fist. During Clinton's eight years in office, the company and Ken Lay contributed about $900,000 to the Democrat party. It also gave $362,000 in soft money donations to Democrats in 1999 and 2000. Since 1996, however, most of Enron's yearly political donations went to the party in power, the Republicans, including heavy contributions to George W. Bush's presidential campaign.[2] Enron didn't play favorites in their attempt to buy favors from greedy politicians; both parties engaged in the hypocrisy of vowing to fight corruption while engaging in the same.

Enron's days were numbered, however. When Enron was forced to admit in 2001 that it had over-reported its profits by nearly $600 million, the corporation imploded, leading to what was the largest bankruptcy in history at that time. Worldcom would later become the largest bankruptcy in history as part of the fallout from the court trials and investigations that followed the Enron scandals.

While Enron was exaggerating its profits, and before its artificially high stock price plummeted, three top executives in the company, Lou Pai,

Kenneth Lay, and Jeff Skilling cashed in stock options worth some $560 million. Like rats on a sinking ship, they got their money out just in time. But, they didn't give that same opportunity to their employees. As the magnitude of the companies' problems became known, Enron's stock crashed, and the company forced more than 12,000 of its employees to retain Enron stock in their 401(k) pension plans. This caused massive losses for the workers at Enron, with many of them losing their entire retirement savings. It was also responsible for the soaring electricity costs and energy shortages that plagued California in 2006.

Further demonstrating the grotesque levels of corporate greed and corruption that had spread like a virus throughout the whole corporation, Enron was also gaming the electricity market and reaping huge speculative profits as an energy wholesaler to California's electricity suppliers. When electricity demand in California rose in 2006, utility companies had no financial incentive to expand production, because wholesalers such as Enron had manipulated the market to force them into daily spot markets for short term gain. It's called megawatt laundering, and Enron executives were masters at it. Basically, companies like Enron buy up electricity in a state like California at below cap price, and then sell it out of state, creating shortages in the state they purchased the electricity from. This creates congestion in the market and drives up prices. The people of California suffered shortages and sky-high prices, but the fat cats at Enron got even richer. When Enron was done robbing the people of California, its appetite for money and influence still not satiated, Ken Lay and his minions robbed their own employees blind as well.

When Charlie Preswood, age sixty-two, retired from Enron after thirty-three years at the company, he thought he had it made. He had amassed $1.3 million dollars in company stock in his 401(k). He had plans to pay off his house and live a comfortable retirement, while leaving an inheritance for his two grown children. Now, however, Preswood finds himself having to sell off parcels of family land to help cover the mortgage and his medical insurance. He runs out of money each month long before he runs out of bills to pay.

More than 20,000 other Enron employees have similar stories. They had been forced to invest in company stock in order to receive matching funds from their employer, and when that employer went bankrupt, making its once valuable stock worth just pennies, they all lost big.

Employees point to a one-month period in the fall of 2001 when they were not allowed to sell their shares of company stock at the same time that executives in the company were rescuing their ill-gotten gains by dumping stock before the ship hit bottom. "It was just terrible," said Roy Rinard, fifty-eight, an Oregon-based lineman for Enron-acquired PGE. Rinard's pension, once worth $470,000, was worth $2,400 when he was finally able to cash it in. He had planned to retire at age sixty, but now faces at least seven more years of grueling work as a lineman before he can afford to retire. "What keeps you going is the fact that you can retire and finally get some rest," Rinard said. "They've taken that away from us. It was pure greed." Steve Lacy, a twenty-five year veteran of PGE, added, "It's just not right to have to watch guys in their early sixties climb poles for a living because someone else stole."[3]

All because of the greed of a few powerful men at the helm of a corporation skilled in bribing politicians and hiding their many sins, thousands of people suffered and lost everything.

RICHES CORRUPT EVERYBODY WHO IS IN THE LEAST CORRUPTIBLE

Unfortunately, the tale of greed in America is not limited just to Enron. Perhaps the greatest single act of greed has occurred over the last number of years right under the noses of the SEC and countless other government organizations who were supposedly watching out for our best interest. Does the name Bernard Madoff ring a bell? This man single handedly created a 50 billion, yes that's BILLION dollar Ponzi scheme that virtually put untold numbers of people into bankruptcy. Why did he do it, because he could and he liked the lavish, high-rolling lifestyle! Yes, he is in prison but the list of financially ruined lives is long and distinguished. All for the love of money!

During every election cycle, we hear countless speeches from politicians assuring us, for instance, that they too are concerned about the rising cost of prescription medication. The public hears their soaring rhetoric repeated often enough that it finally becomes like background noise in the static of rehashed campaign promises. People have a tendency to relegate such noise to the back of their minds with the other issues of the day that will never be dealt with, never be fixed, and will be recycled in the next election and the next campaign. Politicians have succeeded in kicking the can further down the road, and thus the pharmaceutical industry in this country remains another story of greed and corruption that affects millions of people on a daily basis.

THE BIG PRESCRIPTION DRUG RIP-OFF

The American people continue to pay, by far, the highest prices in the world for prescription drugs. This is despite the fact that the U.S. government contributes more money to the development of new drugs than any other government in the world. Nine of the largest pharmaceutical corporations are based in the United States, yet drugs are more expensive in the U.S. than anywhere else, and global drug companies make the bulk of their profits off of the American people.[4]

Many of the exact same drugs sold in the United States are sold abroad at a fraction of the price. This is because pharmaceutical companies have succeeded in blocking drug price regulation in the United States, and have successfully blocked legislation that would allow the importation of drugs from other countries like Canada. Other countries impose price caps on their pharmaceutical companies, while allowing open trade to promote competition and lower prices. Why would a country like America, normally a champion of the free market system and capitalism, allow drug companies to make their own rules and create a monopoly on the market? As with so many things in government, it all goes back to greed.

In the past seven years, the pharmaceutical and health products industry has spent more than $800 million in federal lobbying and campaign donations at the federal and state levels. Its lobbying operation is the biggest in the nation. No other industry in this country spends more money to sway public policy, and buy off politicians than do the drug companies. In 2003, when President George W. Bush signed the Medicare Modernization Act, the drug industry spent nearly $116 million lobbying the government, and it paid off.[5] Drug lobbyists succeeded in getting a provision in the law which barred the Medicare program from negotiating with companies for lower prices. That's your government at work. They line their own pockets, fill their campaign coffers, and make sure the American people will foot the bill for their greed. The next time you hear a politician telling you he feels your pain, and he promises to lower drug costs for hurting Americans, don't believe him. Once they have your vote secured, they will likely go to work for the lobbyists in Washington, and forget every promise they made.

In response to criticism, the drug industry will argue that it requires a great deal of money to fund the research and development of new medications, therefore they are justified in fighting against price regulation, and only do so to fund further research and save lives. I'm afraid their reasons aren't quite so noble. If what they claim is true, why do these companies spend 2.5 times as much on marketing and administration as they do on research and development? They do so because they aren't really doing all of the research. At least a third of the drugs marketed by industry leaders were actually discovered by universities or small biotech companies who will receive only a tiny fraction of the royalties for the drugs they discover. The major drug companies agree to pay something less than 1 percent of the royalties, and then they turn around and sell these new drugs to the public at inflated prices, and ask the very people they are ripping off to cover their phony, massive R&D costs.[6]

GREED GLANDS OUT OF CONTROL

While millions of Americans suffer, and some die, because they are unable to afford the medications they need, the pharmaceutical industry remains the most profitable industry in our country. In 2007, drug company profits exceeded $30 billion. As many elderly citizens cut their dosages in half because they cannot afford to take the dosage prescribed for them by their doctors, five executives at the top pharmaceutical corporations received $706.2 million in stock options in 2000. That was on top of the $134.7 million in wages, bonuses and other compensation they also received. Corporate greed leaves old people suffering so that these FIVE — FIVE! — drug company CEOs can get over a billion dollars in compensation![7]

This kind of gross disparity can continue, despite strong public awareness that it exists, because the pharmaceutical industry is the wealthiest political lobby in Washington, spending more than $200 million in the last three years on campaign contributions, lobbying activities and media advertising. The political influence this money secures makes sure that drug prices stay high, that people cannot import lower-priced drugs from Canada, and that they get access to government-sponsored medical research worth billions of dollars in future profits, all at the taxpayer's expense.

Corporate greed doesn't end with Enron and the pharmaceutical companies, either. It is endemic in our society today. Much of that greed can be traced to its roots in the halls of our government, where the creeping tentacles of greed and corruption have weaved their way into the fabric of our legislative branch, and corrupted once honorable men and women with a lust for power and more money. America is shifting ever closer to the European model of socialism, and greed has driven many Americans to accept a nanny state in place of the self-sufficiency that used to be the life blood of our Republic.

GOVERNMENT GREED

In today's world of politics, Americans work hard, make more money, achieve the American dream, and then politicians take credit for "managing" us into prosperity. It is we, the American people, who created government surpluses in the nineties, yet our leaders act as if it is their money, and they created it for us. Therefore, they feel entitled to keep it, spend it hand-over-fist, and have the temerity to act generous when they give a tiny portion of it back to us in the form of a "rebate". By accepting the liberal establishment's class warfare and victim mentality, we have given up a right to our money, and handed it to the government, blindly believing that the government's purpose is to manage our money, and take care of us. In turn, greedy politicians have gotten more greedy and corrupt, and our prosperity simply breeds more and more government greed.

Our government has done such a fine job of taking our money and "managing" it for us, that, as of this writing, we are in one of the worst financial crises since the Great Depression. The financial crisis of 2008 and the collapse of the housing market is a perfect example of the political greed, combined with our own greed and sense of entitlement that has brought our country to a tipping point financially.

Regardless how hard the media tries to blame the Bush administration for the economic downturn, the beginning of this financial crisis goes back a long way, and has just as many ties to Democrats and President Obama as it does the Republicans.

In the 1990s, if you were barely making a living, had debt running out your ears, and a credit rating a loan officer would laugh at, politicians and lobbying groups were eager to fight for your "right" to get a home loan — and, hopefully, your vote. Politicians used earmarks and pork-barrel spending to fund groups like ACORN (Association of Community Organizers for Reform Now) who were made up of "community organizers" and activists willing to fight for your right to get a loan that you have no hope of being able to repay. You know the government is up to no good when they start assigning you rights you never had before, instead of trying to take rights away, as is their usual modus operandi.

AND THEN THERE WAS ACORN

President Obama was instrumental in pushing for additional assistance for ACORN, and they became a force to be reckoned with in the housing and banking industries. Obama's close friend and associate from his days as a community organizer with ACORN, Madeline Talbott, personally led

Chicago's ACORN campaign to intimidate banks into making high-risk loans to low-credit customers. Protests were held outside the homes of Bank managers, threats were made, boycotts were formed, and ACORN basically bullied the financial system into the whole sub-prime mess that led to a global financial crisis. Banks agreed to lower their credit standards, and give money to ACORN for finance "counseling" operations that would supposedly ensure the new home owners paid back their mortgage loan. The record number of home foreclosures that necessitated a government bailout of the housing market in 2008 tells us how well ACORN's counseling operations worked.

ACORN played a far larger role in creating a financial mess than the media has been willing to report, probably to spare their candidate in the 2008 election, and now their president, the embarrassment of having yet another shady relationship to explain. It was also ACORN that succeeded in drawing Fannie Mae and Freddie Mac, along with sympathetic congressional Democrats, into the very policies that led to financial disaster.[8]

ACORN wasn't just good at community organizing. They have long had very good lobbyists working for them who know how the legislative game is played. And, why not? They were trained by the consummate politician, Barack Obama, when he taught classes for ACORN during his time as a community organizer. While ACORN was harassing bank managers, and generally blackmailing the banking industry into risking everything, they were also using the Community Reinvestment Act of 1977 (CRA), which called on banks to increase lending in poor and minority neighborhoods, to stall bank mergers by filing CRA complaints. Because banks were required to compile public records for home loans into categories like race, gender, and income, ACORN was able to manipulate this data, and embarrass banks into lowering their credit standards. They were so effective at filing these complaints that they were actually able to stop bank mergers and seriously disrupt a bank's ability to do business.

The saga of ACORN is unraveling, the story of greed gone amuck is astonishing. What is yet to be revealed is mind-boggling. Stay tuned.

FANNIE AND FREDDIE ARRIVE ON THE SCENE

ACORN's tactics were amazingly effective in the beginning, however, it was soon realized that working from the outside wasn't going to be enough to satisfy their goals. Bullying banks only got them so far, so they set their sights on Fannie Mae and Freddie Mac, two government-sponsored entities that buy up mortgages and sell them to investors. Using the same tactics, they put pressure on Fannie and Freddie to lower their credit standards. They were met with far greater resistance, however, and didn't really succeed in changing Fannie and Freddie's policies until they gained the backing of several Democrat Senators.

Politicians began to see ACORN as the champions of affordable housing for low income families, and campaign slogans danced before their eyes. Being the experts in class warfare that they are, they saw their opportunity to solidify their base and use affordable housing as a campaign tool. Soon, Congress was making deals with Fannie and Freddie that would convince them to buy high-risk loans against their previous better judgment. In 2003, Barney Frank (D-Mass), chair of the House Financial Services Committee, openly described the "arrangement" this way: "Fannie Mae and Freddie Mac have played a very useful role in helping to make housing more affordable…a mission that this Congress has given them in return for some of the arrangements which are of some benefit to them to focus on affordable housing." If Fannie and Freddie would focus on low-income loans, their Congressional backing and support was secure.[9] This support was especially important to Fannie and Freddie after being damaged by a number of accounting scandals in 2003 and 2004. Senate Democrats also threatened Fannie and Freddie with more restrictive legislation if they didn't cooperate. ACORN won the battle when it was eventually allowed to actually redraft Fannie and Freddie's loan guidelines!

ACORN enjoyed the support of the Clinton Administration as well, who met with them on a monthly basis during the nineties, and they actually gained an ally in the very banking industry they had once protested. Banks found themselves in a position where they now needed Fannie and Freddie to loosen their standards in order to buy their own ACORN-promoted, high risk loans. During the Clinton years, Congress set quotas for low-income housing loans, and Fannie and Freddie went along with it to protect themselves from Congressional threats. ACORNs leaders in the nineties worked with Fannie and Freddie to create the pilot programs that gave us the sub-prime loans that were at the heart of the financial crisis of 2008. Politicians reaped the political benefits, and touted their new programs that would make mortgages available to customers "who have historically been excluded from home ownership". In other words, people who had no earthly business buying a home, because they'd never be able to repay it when the once low rates finally reset and their mortgages went up, became home-owners anyway. That's exactly what we saw happen during the presidential election of 2008, when foreclosures hit an all-time high. The very programs that Senator Obama and his fellow Democrats had helped to establish created the financial crisis that probably got him elected.[10]

PLAYING THE "GREEDY GAME"

This is how the game is now played in this country. Greedy politicians cooperate, or blackmail, greedy corporations with the help of greedy activist groups and greedy lobbyists to create a crisis, and then they present themselves as the saviors who will rescue greedy voters that feel they are entitled to own a home, whether they can afford it or not. The greed comes full circle. Well, almost. There's another level of greed that our legislative branches of government, state and federal, have made into an art. It manifests itself in the form of "pork barrel spending", "pay to play deals", campaign contributions with strings attached, and tax increases that are squandered on political favors and Congressional pay raises.

Legislation is increasingly defined by the hundreds of pages of earmarks allocating our tax dollars to pay for such things as the infamous "bridge to nowhere" in Alaska. Earmarks also fund things like grape research in New York, and the research of new uses for wood. What follows is but a small taste of the kind of senseless earmarks that are inserted into legislation, often times without the knowledge of those who are voting for the legislation.[11]

PORK-BARREL SPENDING AND EARMARKS

1. $2 million to the NAVY for "waterless urinals".

2. $1 million to John Murtha's non-existent recipients (Murtha did not defend the challenge to his non-existent recipients, and the earmark was dropped).

3. $1 million for the Hillary Clinton's "Hippie" museum to honor Woodstock.

4. $500,000 for the Sparta Teapot Museum.

5. $13.5 million to an Irish group that funds the World Toilet Summit.

6. $300,000 to analyze bear fur.

7. $1.3 million for Raleigh, North Carolina to build a year round, "climate-controlled" park carousel.

8. $63 million in unspent earmarks for the Michigan Dept. of Transportation (the earmarks will be absorbed by the federal government).

These are just a small sampling. As you can see, greed has become the primary motivation for much of our society, and its partner corruption has already brought devastation and hardship down on the entire country. Yet, we may still have a greater price to pay, if we don't change course and hold our government to account. President Obama promised to bring transparency to government. He further promised to use his line by line veto right to cut any earmarks. He lied to Americans and has refused to do either of the above. What say you who voted for this fraud?

GOD IS WATCHING

Many evangelicals hold as their primary concern the possibility that America will collapse from immorality, sexual perversion, theological liberalism, or cold churches. These are definitely matters we should all be concerned about, but the Bible indicates that we may need to adjust our priorities when it comes to healing our nation. You may not realize how often the Word of God calls down the judgment of Almighty God on leaders and nations that embody the very grip of greed we see in American democracy today.   Consider the blistering words of Amos, the prophet of justice:

> *Hear this, you who trample the needy and do away with the poor of the land, saying, "When will the New Moon be over that we may sell grain, and the Sabbath be ended that we may market wheat?" — skimping the measure, boosting the price and cheating with dishonest scales, buying the poor with silver and the needy for a pair of sandals, selling even the sweepings with the wheat. The LORD has sworn by the Pride of Jacob: "I will never forget anything they have done. Will not the land tremble for this, and all who live in it mourn? The whole land will rise like the Nile; it will be stirred up and then sink like the river of Egypt". "In that day," declares the Sovereign LORD, "I will make the sun go down at noon and darken the earth in broad daylight. I will turn your religious feasts into mourning and all your singing into weeping. I will make all of you wear sackcloth and shave your heads. I will make that time like mourning for an only son and the end of it like a bitter day." (Amos 8:4-10)*

The days of Amos were not altogether unlike our days. The capital of the Northern Kingdom at Samaria had experienced a bubble of economic growth and luxurious living. Much like our own dot com bubble, or any one of many real estate bubbles our society has weathered, this bubble was about to burst. God was not locked up somewhere in the Temple in Jerusalem. He was out there in the marketplace watching every transaction, making note of every dirty deed. God describes in these verses the rapaciously greedy "church-goers" of Amos' day licking their lips and rubbing their hands together; they cannot wait for religious observances to be over so they might go out and defraud their poor fellow-citizens with false weights and measures. For a little silver they would sell the poor. They did not consider a poor person worth more than a pair of shoes.

God makes a striking statement concerning this kind of corporate greed. He will never forget it. That sobering statement should cause all of us to take pause. I have not seen mentioned in Scripture any other national sin that God will never forget. He swears by the excellency of Jacob that He will never forget the greed that savaged the poor and helpless people of Samaria. God promises floods, a trembling earth, and even utter darkness at midday for such a nation. Yet, the greedy covetous men of Samaria were rank amateurs compared to what is unfolding before our very eyes in America today. If God overlooks this unrepentant greed, He will have to apologize to the Israel of old on judgment day.

The greed demonstrated in modern America has nothing remotely to do with any actual unmet need of contemporary Americans today. Enron, WorldCom, AIG and all the rest demonstrate the demonic quality of greed beyond need. It belongs to the mystery of iniquity.

Augustine of HippoRegius, the so-called Saint Augustine of Christian history, wrote a famous book of personal testimony in which he tried to understand the psychology of his own greed. He reflected for a long time on the theft of a pear when he was only a lad. He puzzled that he was not hungry, did not need the pear and, indeed, had access to plenty of better pears. Yet he stole the pear. He struggled with the overmastering craving for something he did not in any sense need. We've all struggled with this same senseless greed and covetousness.

Before we point our accusing finger at the CEOs of greedy corporations, we would do well to look into our own hearts. To what extent are we driven by the demon of greed? How much of our own lives say to those around us, enough is never enough? We don't want to drive that Taurus or Honda. Instead, we are feverish until we can get a BMW or Lexus. If we have a 2,000 square foot, adequate home in an older suburb, we chaff until we can go head-over-heels in debt for a 4,000 square foot home that is largely unoccupied most of the day. We would rather buy the same clothes at Neiman Marcus than Wal-mart. Our children insist on the latest trendy gadget when we may not have enough money to buy their school clothes and school supplies. Is not the greed of corporate America simply our own petty greed writ large against a corporate screen?

Greed always contains the seeds of its own self-destruction. The fable of King Midas exemplifies that truth. When granted one wish, Midas wished that everything he touched would instantly turn to gold. His wish was granted and he was soon surrounded by gold. He would be rich beyond his wildest dreams! That is, until he touched his own favorite daughter. His greedy touch left her forever frozen in gold, and the king lost that which was most precious to him.

As American troops began their retreat from the island of Corregidor during the Japanese campaign for the conquest of the Philippines during World War II, they needed to destroy the United States currency that was held for their future pay in the vast tunnel networks under the island. Faced with almost certain starvation, and not wanting the money to fall into the hands of the Japanese, they lit their GI cigarettes with the bills that would be of no use to them in the Prisoner of War camps they would soon occupy. How quickly life can seem more important than stuff.

A Texas farm woman owned a large ranch in North Texas. She was famous for her penurious and grasping spirit. Both she and her little grand-daughter collected "Green Stamps" trading stamps. Her granddaughter needed only one more book of stamps to trade for a favorite toy, so she asked her granny for the stamps. Grandma refused. When an outraged family member asked the greedy old woman whether or not she thought she would take it with her, she replied, "I just might." Well, the fact is, she did not. You'll never see a hearse with a U-Haul on it, and granny didn't take a single green stamp with her. Occasionally, someone at a funeral will ask me quietly how much the deceased left. My answer is always the same. Everything.

THE SORDID HISTORY

Surely one of the most dramatic stories in the sordid history of human greed is that of Ahab, king of Israel, as told in 1 Kings, chapter 21. A wealthy king with a luxurious palace at Samaria, Ahab lived a life of wealth beyond the wildest imagination of his subjects. In stark contrast, a poor man named Naboth lived meagerly on the tiny patch of land, adjacent to a royal estate in Jezreel, that made up his family's vineyard. Naboth was not greedy for his own vineyard. In fact, it was the specific command of God in the Old Testament that a Hebrew was not supposed to give up his patrimony (Lev. 25:23; Num. 36:7). Rather than seek more for himself elsewhere, he kept the patrimony of his family in humble obedience to God, a law Ahab must certainly have known himself. The greedy king, however, cared neither for God nor man. Ahab lusted for the tiny plot of the humble Hebrew Naboth. In response to her husband's covetousness, Ahab's wicked, pagan wife, the infamous Jezebel, arranged on her weak husband's behalf to have Naboth murdered. Jez would make Lady MacBeth look like the president of the women's circle!

Enter the prophet Elijah with a word from God. Elijah prophesied that, in the very place of his unfettered greed, Ahab would die. He warned the king that "in the place where dogs licked the blood of Naboth, dogs shall lick your blood, even yours'" (1 King 21:19). Time passed. Every time a dog barked, Ahab jumped! More time passed. Ahab finally began to relax, and forgot about the prophecy. Then still more time passed. Much later, Ahab found himself in battle. He tried to pass himself off as a commoner to save his neck, and it worked for a time. But, God always gets his man. In a random act of violence, 1 Kings 22:34 tells us that "a certain man drew a bow at random, and struck the king of Israel between the joints of his armor." Think of that. An aimless shot at an unknown man carried with it the judgment of God on a greedy king. Wounded and dying, the king ordered that his chariot driver rush him back to Samaria. As they traveled, the king's blood ran into the bottom of the chariot and out on to the streets of Samaria, where, as was prophesied, the wild mongrel dogs licked it up in their ravenous hunger, greedy for the blood of the greedy king.

In the very place of his lustful greed, Ahab died the death of a judged man. How many a millionaire has died alone in his mansion, abandoned by his many wives and random children. All of his money could not buy him a single friend at his death.

One of the most famous pastors in American history stated late in his life a truth learned at the helm of a wealthy church: "Great wealth brings great misery."

Queen Elizabeth I of England cried on her deathbed, "My kingdom for an inch of time." Even though she mixed her metaphors, we understand her meaning. She would give all she had for more time.

THE SUM OF IT ALL

My friend, look into your own heart for the evidence of greed. Covetousness, envy, unhindered lust for more and more — these will not only destroy your life, they will bring down our great nation. The United States of America was not built on the shifting sands of greed. As was explained at the outset of this chapter, to this day Americans willingly give a larger percent of their disposable income to charity than the people of any other nation on the face of the earth. Yet, we also find the greatest examples of fraudulent greed taking place all around us. God will not be mocked. He has set his face against arrogant greed.

America is at a tipping point in so many areas, and greed tops the list of our national sins. As God clearly warned, that is a precarious position to be in as a people. So, let liberality and generosity, openhandedness, bigheartedness, bounteousness and kindness flow from your life. When you draw your last breath, you will never regret the generosity of your life, and you will have helped save our nation from the judgment of God.

CHAPTER SIX

THE CULTURE OF DEATH
Abortion: The Greatest Scandal
Confronting America's Social Conscience

*There are choices to be made in every
age. And who we are depends on the
choices we make. What will our choices
be? What boundaries will we uphold to
make it possible for people to say with
certainty that moral atrocities are truly
evil. Which side will we be on?*

Dr. Frances Schaeffer
Whatever Happened to the Human Race

Every year more than 1,500,000 — that's one million five hundred thousand — babies are denied life in this country. Worldwide the number is a staggering 42 Million! Since 1973 the number in America stands at more than 50 million alive, yet unborns have been murdered! This chapter and the appendices referenced will expose, in heartrending detail, the truth about the horrific practice of abortion. America now lives in a culture of death where the death cult has a greater evangelistic outreach than the Church, and where there is a growing political power that threatens to force their worldview on the rest of us, as well as those we love and care about. America is at yet another tipping point.

Abortion remains the greatest scandal confronting America's social conscience and yet it remains further from resolution than at any moment since the Roe v. Wade decision was handed down in 1973. Why is that?

Why has this not been overturned? Why does this remain such a contentious moral issue when even the latest Gallup poll tells the story? The headline of this report should encourage pro-life Americans: *"More Americans Pro-Life than Pro-Choice."* That is so telling when 51 percent of those polled indicated that they are "pro-life." That percentage has gone up five points since the last poll which was 46 percent in August 2001 and May 2002. Additional polling by the Gallup organization confirmed its findings and revealed startling other information showing that Americans are really confused by the abortion question, and it is deeper now than at any point since 1973. Americans are genuinely squeamish about abortion, and we all should be.

Moral Relativism has had its most devastating affect on our society by lowering our standards to the point where the value of human life has been and is being greatly diminished. A measurable percentage of the population would protest the death penalty for a mass murderer because they believe it is inhumane, yet they have such a malfunctioning moral compass that they, at the same time defend the murder of an innocent baby in the womb. They would, likewise, feel no guilt or shame for supporting the starvation of another human being, as long as a doctor has decided that the human being's life is no longer worth living, especially if a doctor determines that person has become a burden on society and their family. Much like the Nazi's in Germany, or the Communist government in China, the greater good is served by eliminating the burden of a cancer patient's medical costs with a cocktail of lethal drugs administered by a doctor. As I will demonstrate in this chapter, our fellow humans have become just another animal in Darwin's evolutionary drama.

THE SLAUGHTER OF THE INNOCENTS: WHAT REALLY HAPPENS IN ABORTION CLINICS

An abortion is a procedure, usually done in an abortion clinic or a hospital by a licensed doctor, with the goal of intentionally ending a pregnancy. When a mother enters the abortion clinic to have an abortion, she is not carrying within her a mass of nonliving tissue but a developing child that has its own heartbeat. Her baby's heartbeat is visible on an ultrasound, and depending on when the abortion is done, he or she may resemble in many ways the child that will leave the birth canal when gestation is complete. Because abortions are performed at different stages of pregnancy, there are different methods of killing the baby. The media tries to soften abortion rhetoric, so you may not be used to hearing it put in these harsh terms. But, I believe as you read the specifics of how a baby develops during the different stages of pregnancy, and what happens to the baby during an abortion, you will agree with me that abortion can only accurately be described as brutally killing an innocent child. These procedures and photos can be viewed in the back of this book if you wish to go there now. (Read Appendix 3, but be prepared to feel revulsion and a lot of other emotions.)

The largest group of American citizens, therefore, to become a victim of this morbid acceptance of death as natural has been the unborn, through the legalization of abortion, and the desensitization of the population to its horrors. Where abortion is too horrific even for many of the most faithful in the death cult, disinformation and censorship is used to hide the facts and protect us from the gory details of what we are really doing, or allowing by our silence to happen. But, before we look at the politics and deception involved in the abortion movement, I want you the reader to understand what, exactly, an abortion is, and what abortionists are really referring to when they speak of the "fetus" that is destroyed in the process of an abortion. One of the tactics of the abortion industry, and those who believe infanticide should be the right of every woman, is to keep this information from being widely known by the general population. This cannot be emphasized often enough. They demonize those who try to present the facts, as if the true immorality lies with those who feel people have a right to know the gory, barbaric reality of what abortion is before they decide to support it. They know well that the American people are kind and compassionate people who would never support the abortion industry if they were made aware of what really happens in their death centers.

In truth, the American people don't actually support abortion anywhere near to the extent the media would have us believe. A nationwide survey done by the U.S. Conference of Catholic Bishops showed that 82 percent of American adults think that abortion should be either illegal under all circumstances or with limited legality, and only 9 percent said that abortion should be legal for any reason at any time during pregnancy.[1] The vast majority of Americans are in complete disagreement with Planned Parenthood's position that abortion should be an unlimited right of every woman. The following is a list of some of findings of this survey that may surprise you:

1. 95 percent favor laws ensuring that abortions be performed only by licensed physicians

2. 88 percent favor informed consent laws (i.e., that require abortion providers to inform women of potential risks to their physical and psychological health and about alternatives to abortion. The abortion movement and Planned Parenthood appose this simple compromise)

3. 76 percent favor laws that protect doctors and nurses from being forced to perform or refer for abortions against their will

4. 73 percent favor laws that require giving parents the chance to be involved in their minor daughter's abortion decisions. (Some states actually make it illegal for parents to be notified against their children's wishes. Ironically, there are laws on the books prohibiting children from receiving even an aspirin at school without parental notification, and minors must have the permission of their parents to get their ears pierced in many states.[2])

5. 68 percent favor laws against partial-birth abortion (i.e. aborting a child already partially delivered from the mother)

6. 63 percent favor laws preventing the use of taxpayer funds for abortions

The latest to jump on board voicing approval of abortion is an Anglican priest, the Dean of the Episcopal Divinity School in Cambridge, Massachusetts. The Rev. Katherine Hancock Ragsdale, speaking in Birmingham, Alabama, declared abortion to be "a blessing and abortionists are doing holy work." She also thinks that the people who run abortion clinics are "heroes" and even "saints." Does she not know the Sixth Commandment?

And then there are the Friends of the Earth and the Greenpeaces of this world who are now urging that environmentalists everywhere push for a two-child limit, and that abortion be used to save the environment. Never mind that children won't be saved; it is of more importance that governments must reduce population growth through better family planning. Did I hear someone say "Sounds like China."

Has no one ever heard of the Sixth Commandment which says, "Thou shalt not murder" (Ex. 20:13). Alan Redpath, well-known pastor and author of many much-appreciated Christian books, in *Law and Liberty: The Ten Commandments for Today,* states that he wishes those four words from the Sixth Commandment, could appear like fire in the sky so that all may recognize the sovereignty of God over human life. However, that's not God's way of speaking. He has spoken in His Son, and Jesus is His last word to mankind (Heb. 1:1-2).

Like Redpath, we, who call ourselves Christians, should pray that the Holy Spirit might enable us to proclaim this Commandment in the light of its Old Testament setting, and also in its New Testament significance, in such a way that we may feel the force of it in our hearts and lives, and then that it may reach and speak through us to others. So be it, Lord.

LOBBYISTS, GREEDY POLITICIANS, MAINSTREAM MEDIA DISINFORMATION CAMPAIGNS, AND WELL-ORGANIZED GROUPS LIKE PLANNED PARENTHOOD

So, how is it that abortion remains legal, parental consent or notification is often forbidden, and even partial birth abortion has been difficult to ban in this country? The answer is summed up in this — lobbyists with a lot of money, greedy politicians, and judges who legislate from the bench. Congress continues to pass laws making abortions easier to get, because pro-abortion lobbyists make the same behind-the-scenes deals as the pharmaceutical industry to influence our lawmakers, and buy votes for their cause.

There is never a shortage of greedy politicians ready to fill their campaign coffers with the bribes from lobbyists. When Congress fails to thwart the will of the people, and voters successfully limit abortions through state referendums, activist judges ignore the will of the people, and rule these referendums unconstitutional.

The mainstream media and groups like Planned Parenthood have also engaged in a propaganda campaign that has left many Americans feeling alone in their beliefs that abortion should be illegal. How many times have you heard news reporters and pundits pontificate about the will of the American people, as if their personal views represent that of most Americans, whether supported by the facts or not? I'm not sure if knowing the truth about the majority view would motivate the public to actually contact their representatives in government, and put forth the same energy, effort and money that the minority has been able to generate in furthering the pro-choice movement, but the successful disinformation campaign surrounding public support for abortion certainly hasn't helped the pro-life cause.

Despite overwhelming public support for limiting, and even banning some kinds of abortion, the number of abortions performed in this country has grown to staggering levels. As stated at the outset of this chapter, as of 2007, nearly 50 million abortions have been performed in the United States since 1973.[3] That's million!

Fifty million human beings have been denied the right to live the life God had intended for them. Sometimes this was because the parents found having a child inconvenient. In other instances because of a disability or deformity the parents felt made their child's life not worth living, and in a miniscule number of cases, because the baby was unfortunate enough to be conceived due to rape or incest. I find it most disturbing that babies with Down syndrome are, more often than not, aborted because their parents, for whatever reason, don't want to care for a special needs child. Anyone who has known someone with Down syndrome knows the unconditional love that these children of God display, and the joy and happiness they bring to their families and all those who know them. It is a tragedy that we are so often denied their contribution to the world.

The pro-abortion movement in this country has become so increasingly militant in their promotion of abortion, that they maliciously attack women verbally who choose to have their handicapped babies rather than kill them in the womb. An example of this can be found in the attacks on Sarah Palin, Senator McCain's Vice Presidential running mate in the 2008 Presidential election. Palin, already a mother of four, and a successful Governor of Alaska, became pregnant in her forties with a child that she and her husband Todd would later learn had Down syndrome. The Palins' pro-life beliefs were more than just mere words on a bumper sticker, and they did not just talk the talk, they walked the walk. Palin chose to carry her baby to term, and her baby boy, Trigg, was born four months before she was picked to run for Vice President of the United States.

In the eyes of the media and liberal abortion supporters, this career woman had not only chosen to have an unplanned, or in their terminology an "unwanted" pregnancy, but she had dared to give birth to a child with special needs. Newscasters criticized her for not aborting a disabled child that would, in their opinion, have a difficult life ahead of "it." I heard newscasters actually refer to baby Trigg as "it" on numerous occasions, and it never occurred to them that they were referring to a living, breathing baby boy, not a subhuman "it." Seeing Palin on a stage before millions of television viewers, proudly holding baby Trigg following the Vice Presidential debate, stirred in them the guilt that they work so hard to suppress. They refer to the unborn as an embryo or fetus, and describe an abortion as nothing more than the removal of fetal tissue. The abortion terminology they use is designed to avoid any human traits or characteristics in describing the baby. When, during the Vice Presidential debate, Palin's daughter Piper was seen holding baby Trigg, licking her fingers, and smoothing out Trigg's hair so that he would look nice for the camera, they were forced to acknowledge that what would have been aborted, if left to them, was a sweet, innocent child, loved by his siblings, and cherished by his parents.

I believe that much of the unfair and, in fact, unprecedented attacks on such an accomplished and talented woman were, in large part, because she served a crushing blow to the abortion industry's lie that some babies are better off dead. She became a voice for all women who choose to have their babies, no matter the challenges that come with it, and she drew attention to the ugly realities of what abortion is. The pro-death crowd loves to frame themselves as the champions of a woman's right to choose, but in truth, they only believe in a woman's right to choose, if she chooses to have an abortion.

THE HYPOCRISY OF THE PRO-ABORTION MOVEMENT

The hypocrisy of the pro-abortion movement is one thing, but to fully understand the evil involved in their industry of death, one must fully understand what an abortion is. Planned Parenthood and groups like them are very careful to couch the debate in delicate terms that make an abortion sound like a simple, painless procedure that injures no one. The death procedure is portrayed as no more than a minor inconvenience for the mother. Nothing could be farther from the truth. Depending on the stage of pregnancy the mother is in when the abortion is performed, the procedure is a progressively gruesome and horrific act of brutality on an innocent baby. What you can read about in the appendix will at times be graphic, and may be unsettling, but it is important to know the truth about this holocaust on our society. Too many Christians and non-Christians alike are uninformed about these truths, and therefore less effective in changing hearts and minds when the opportunity arises. Christians must be the moral compass for this nation, and it is so important for us to engage in the debate and do all we can to end this brutal practice. The lives of literally millions of children depend on you and me.

MARGARET SANGER AND PLANNED PARENTHOOD: "WEEDING OUT THE UNFIT"

Because the pro-abortion movement has worked so hard to distance itself from past evils and associations, few people know about the true history of Planned Parenthood, the abortion movement, and the founder of Planned Parenthood Federation of America, Margaret Sanger. There is a very good reason for burying this history, as we shall see.

While Eugenics is often associated with Europe and the rise in popularity of Darwinism, as well as Hitler's fancy for this form of race cleansing, it's important to note here that the science of Eugenics was popular in both America and Europe during the early 1900s. As hard as it might be for some to believe, because it's a part of American history rarely discussed, tens of thousands of people in America were subjected to forced sterilizations during the 1920s and 1930s. The Eugenics Society of America was quite successful during these decades in convincing many Americans that the disabled, the "morons" as they called them, the idiots, the epileptics, and the mentally ill should not be allowed to procreate. Drawing on Darwin's theory of natural selection and its pillar of, "the survival of the fittest", Eugenicists believed that for the betterment of humanity, and so that we might evolve into a better human race, the weak must die off, and be prevented from tainting the gene pool. The goal was to prevent the weaker less productive people in society from propagating any more of "their kind," and thereby creating a master race of more perfect people that would continue to evolve as nature had intended them to. Sounds an awful lot like Hitler's defense for his Eugenics plan, doesn't it? There's a reason they sound similar.

In 1876 scientists began to believe that criminality was genetic. In other words, criminals were programmed for crime. Eugenicists believed that since criminal tendencies were inherited, they should strive to curtail the breeding of groups that produce criminals. By the early 1930s, thirty states in the U.S. had sterilization laws, and by 1958, 60,000 Americans had been sterilized, many against their will.[8] Later, when the Nazi's forcibly sterilized the "unfit" in their program to create a master race, they claimed to be acting, like America, on "biological principles." Hitler even claimed that he had studied the laws of several American states for the sterilization of people whose breeding was "injurious to the racial stock."[9]

After Germany was defeated and Hitler's eugenics program exposed and discredited, leading eugenicists in America turned to contraception and abortion as a method of population control, and as a way of avoiding the stigma that Hitler had brought on their current programs and methods.

These scientists and eugenics proponents liked to link Darwin's theory of natural selection with what they called "voluntary parenthood."

Enter Margaret Sanger, the founder of Planned Parenthood and the Planned Parenthood Federation of America (PPFA). When Sanger founded Planned Parenthood in 1916, it is clear that she was very much a supporter of eugenics. She believed that birth control could serve a great purpose to the human race by keeping what she described as the "genetically unfit" from reproducing.

In her 1920 book, *Woman and the New Race*, Sanger explicitly called her work "nothing more or less than the facilitation of the process of weeding out the unfit, of preventing the birth of defectives or those who will become defectives." She also wrote in *The Birth Control Review*, "The most urgent problem today is how to limit and discourage the over-fertility of the mentally and physically defective."[10]

The President of Planned Parenthood from 1962-1974, Alan Guttmacher, was also a eugenicist, and once warned a gathering of Planned Parenthood employees, "The mentally retarded and the mentally defective...insidiously are replacing the people of normal mentality." It wasn't just Sanger and Guttmacher who believed in eugenics, however. Half of the National Council of Sanger's American Birth Control League were prominent eugenicists in the country.

The American Eugenic Society also endorsed Sanger's group in 1932, and Sanger was a member of this group through the 1960s.

Not only would most American's not know this history of the largest abortion provider in the country, but most of Planned Parenthood's employees would not be aware of it either. Sanger's goal of ridding our society of what she deemed the "unfit" can still be seen in the practices and results of Planned Parenthood today. The vast majority of Planned Parenthood's clients have incomes below the poverty line. A 1997 Planned Parenthood "Plan of Action" asserted that its "core clients were young women, low-income women, and women of color." There also remains a bias against those with disabilities. A former employee of PPFA, who had disabilities, told the New York Times that her colleagues "believed there was a need to abort fetuses diagnosed with disabilities. There was a feeling that they were bad babies," she said. "There was a strong eugenics mentality that exhibited disdain, discomfort, and ignorance toward disabled babies."[11]

The eugenics mentality of Planned Parenthood is at the heart of its founding and its purpose even today. Margaret Sanger's grandson even made a case for abortion using a Darwinian defense as recently as 2004, when he asserted that "abortion is good, and we must become proud that we have taken control of our reproduction. This has been a major factor in advancing human evolution and survival."

THE MOTHERS

Before we move on, I want to briefly touch on the affect abortion has on the mothers of these aborted babies. Does their life really get better when they are relieved of the "burden" of carrying their child? Planned Parenthood would have us believe that they are doing these women a wonderful service by giving them a choice. But, the fact is, many of these woman are not given a choice. They are too often coerced by parents, boyfriends, or abortion clinics themselves into getting an abortion. I could cite many stories of young women marched into abortion clinics by their mothers or boyfriends to have a procedure done that will eliminate embarrassment or a potential burden for the mother, and protect the potential father from taking any responsibility for the child he fathered. The would-be young mother is left to bear the depression, the guilt and regret she will feel for the rest of her life.

There is a growing body of evidence that indicates abortions can cause devastating psychological consequences for the mother. A 1989 congressional hearing on the impact of abortion found that people who have abortions "report horrible nightmares of children calling them from trash cans, of body parts, and blood." Psychologist Wanda Franz, Ph.D., testified that "when they are reminded of the abortion, the women re-experienced it with terrible psychological pain …They feel worthless and victimized because they failed at the most natural of human activities — the role of being a mother."[12]

It has been well established that what is now termed Post-Abortion Syndrome (PAS) does exist. In fact, a Los Angeles Times survey in 1989 found that 56 percent of women who had abortions felt guilty about it, and 26 percent regretted the abortion. This fact, unfortunately, has not stopped the abortion industry from successfully promoting the view that they are doing these women a favor, and saving them and their baby a horrible life that no one would want.

Even our current President promoted this view during the 2008 Presidential campaign. At a town hall meeting in Johnstown, Pennsylvania, a member of the audience pleaded with Obama to "stop these abortions." In response, he gave lip service to the miracle of a newborn baby, mentioning his own two precious daughters as an example. He continued the example of his own daughters to make his final point by saying, "Look, I [sic] got two daughters — nine-years old and six-years years old. I am going to teach them first about values and morals, but if they make a mistake, I don't want them punished with a baby." Some values Mr. President! He would teach his daughters that a baby is a punishment, and that it is acceptable to kill that child to correct your own "mistake." Is it any wonder we so cavalierly kill off our young, and place no value on human life with elected leaders like this? Obama's pick for surgeon general in his White House cabinet was a fifty-two-year-old black woman, a family doctor who urged that future doctors in medical schools learn how to perform abortions. As a member of the AMA (American Medical Association), according to the Associated Press, she said, "We are adopting a policy that medical school curriculum provide the legal, ethical and psychological principles associated with abortion so students can learn all the factors involved." So that is the stated policy now of "America's Family Physician."

Much more could be said about the motives of the pro-abortion movement, and the devastating affects it has had on the lives of mothers, families, and of course, the unborn. For the purposes of space, I must move on to the most recent target of the death cult in America. Their plan of ridding the world of the unfit foiled by legislation and the successes of the pro-life movement, the death cult in America has sought to rid us of the "unfit" by other means. If abortionists can't create a master race through abortion, then perhaps they can weed out the unfit and unwanted later in life by "compassionately" killing them. I'm speaking of the Euthanasia movement, also called the right to die movement that has seen some successes in recent legislation, judicial decisions, and voter referendums across the country. It is yet another attack on the innocent and the weakest in our society, and it is the next step in the pro-death movement's campaign to bring about societal change and population control through murder and death.

CHAPTER SEVEN

"THE RIGHT TO DIE"
Eugenicists Find a New Slogan

> *Modern medical technology has developed*
> *remarkable means to prolong our living —*
> *and our dying…[but] Prohibition of the direct*
> *taking of human life, except in self-defense or*
> *in the defense of others, has been a central*
> *tenet of Judeo-Christian tradition and teach-*
> *ing…Human life is a gift of our sovereign*
> *God, who alone is entitled to determine when*
> *and how an individual life will end.*
>
> **Robert D. Orr, M.D., David L. Schiedermayer, M.D.,**
> **David B. Biebel, D.Min.**
> In *Life and Death Decisions*

The advances of the abortion or pro-death movement, and the tacit approval of abortion by uninformed or lazy voters, have led to a natural progression toward another form of population control. With human life devalued, eugenics has reared its ugly head again in the form of mercy killings. Those who support it prefer to call it euthanasia, as if our loved ones are no different than the family pet that has to be euthanized in its old age. Or, they might prefer the right to die. The right to die implies that these people, who will be helped into their grave by doctors and hospices, have a choice in the matter. In many cases, however, they do not, and even their families have no say in the matter. For the weakest among us, a judge is often given the power to decide how and when these people die. One such example sticks out in many American's minds, as it brought into the light a practice that has been going on for some time now, a practice not talked about in print media or on television and radio talk shows to much extent, if at all.

On Easter weekend of 2005 police stood watch over the parents of Terri Schiavo to make sure that they did not touch their daughter's cracked and bleeding lips with any water. Only at the last were they even permitted, by her "husband" Michael Schiavo, to give her Holy Communion on Easter Sunday. As she starved to death and dehydrated because of our government's refusal to give her the same elements society gives to murderers held in prison, the world watched and Congress fulminated in debate. Late-night television viewers were treated to a harangue by Massachusetts homosexual Congressman Barney Frank calling for the United States Congress to agree with the state and federal court system to pull the tube, and starve Terri to death.

In a larger sense, congressional representative Frank embodies the debate surrounding the culture of death in America. He promotes gay lesbian marriage contrary to biblical and natural law. If all people lived like Congressman Frank, society would die from lack of reproduction. Frank supports abortion to terminate life at its beginning. Ironically, at the very time the government was killing Terri Schiavo, that same government banned a mother from rescuing her fourteen-year-old daughter from an abortion clinic that would kill her baby. Frank, obviously, also supported the governmental murder of the disabled, as evidenced by his midnight appeal to the United States Congress to pull the tube on Terri Schiavo.

This is the Barney Frank who wants to save the trees in Alaska and the whales in the Pacific. He belongs to the infamous coalition of tree huggers known for chaining themselves to trees in order to spare the helpless timber an eminent and torturous death. Frank is willing to send Greenpeace boats to save whales and porpoises. Yet, without hesitation, he led the charge for the governmental consent to Terri Schiavo's death.

To add to the moral nausea and spiritual vertigo of the incident, Terri's husband Michael trumped her parents in leading the "kill Terri" parade. To say that he was less than selfless is to state the obvious. He had won a two

MILLION dollar malpractice settlement, ostensibly to keep Terri alive. Within months of winning that legal windfall, he revealed his true desires for Terri when he attempted to keep the doctors from treating a severe infection that threatened her life. Guess who became the recipient of the remaining settlement money after she finally died? You guessed it — Michael, and indirectly his new flame and live-in lover. No wonder he suddenly "remembered," after the settlement was final, that Terri had, in some unrecorded conversation, supposedly requested that she be starved to death. This was contradicted by friends and family who testified in later court appeals that, as a devout Catholic, Terri was politically and morally against any form of assisted suicide or euthanasia. The courts, however, felt more comfortable trusting an abusive husband with millions of dollars to gain by her death, as well as the freedom to marry his live-in lover and mother of his new children, who was also likely waiting for his current wife to die.

Terri Schiavo had allegedly entered into what the culture of death liberals call PVS, a persistent vegetative state. Never mind that this term is not even thirty-years-old, and the condition it describes is not well understood, or scientifically proven to exist as it is defined within the medical community. Never mind that a qualified medical doctor testified that she was in no such condition. Let's just ignore that the mother who conceived her, carried her and gave birth to her, insisted that Terri still enjoyed life and responded to her mother's love. Please don't mention that since time immemorial the dedication of doctors under the Hippocratic Oath has always been the preservation of life, or that the leading, orthodox Catholic, Protestant and Jewish religious leaders called out for the preservation of her life. Let the culture of death reign.

THE INSANE LOSS OF A MORAL COMPASS

How did this insane loss of a moral compass take place? As was stated earlier, it's one of the things you can lay at the feet of Charles Darwin. With the ascent of evolutionary theory, the inevitable loss of respect for human life in the image of God is the outcome. Until Darwin recorded his unproven and improvable theory, Western Civilization believed that humans were created in the *imago dei,* the image of God. This never meant that we looked like God. Any walk through an urban mall would convince you that God must look better than most folks presently walking around. The image of God refers to that unique capacity for relating to God that belongs to man alone. It is not difficult to understand how postmodern society has accorded to trees, and whales, or Fido in the back yard, the same value it gives to humans. If we are all simply winners in the survival of the fittest, there is no distinction between humans and other animals (or trees).

And, so, we are brought to the debate about *euthanasia.* This rather chilling word is a combination of two Greek words, *eu* which means *good* and *thanatos* which means *death.* Good death. Such a concept could only be born in a culture that is post-biblical. The Bible always regards death as an interloper, intruder and enemy. You find no support at all in the Bible for death being a friendly end to the journey of life. Death is punishment for sin which entered the world at the time of original creation with Adam and Eve, our first parents, when they disobeyed God. Death is an end to be avoided at all costs. Death was not God's intention in original creation. Only a morally debased secularism has made death a "natural" end of life. Such a view is Greek/pagan rather than Hebrew/biblical.

Compare the death of Socrates with the death of Jesus. When Socrates was condemned by the Greek city-state of Athens, he gathered his disciples around him and, after a discourse, drank the cup of hemlock as a natural pagan end of his life, wherein his good soul left his bad body. Contrast that with the death of Jesus. In the Garden, Jesus so dreaded the ordeal of His own vicarious death that His sweat glands somehow burst into his arteries and He sweated drops of blood. Hebrews reminds us that He offered Himself up with loud cries. Death was an enemy to Him, an agony caused by the sin of the world.

The liberal naturalist view of death today recaps the view of Greek pagans. Death is a natural friend. There is no spiritual component in death. It is not the penalty of sin, and it is not an eternal state of anguish in Hell. Death for the secularist has become a quiet, natural conclusion of life, and hence something over which the autonomous individual has the right of decision. Death has been made a commodity. Just as there are twenty kinds of apples and seemingly hundreds of kinds of cheeses in a gourmet market, the time and means of death is now a commodity. Who cares? Kill the "tissue" in a mother's womb or kill Terri Schiavo.

THE WARPED WORLDVIEW OF LIFE

This warped worldview has led to the *utilitarian* view of life so obvious in the godless liberals pontificating on Terri's life. They did not ask whether or not her life was a sacred spiritual gift from God, of worth in itself because it came from His hand. They rather asked, "Is she in a position to enjoy life?" In their arrogance, these lovers of choice appointed themselves the judge and jury that would decide for Terri what made her life enjoyable.

As this book is being written, Obama and his top health advisors, are agreeing with him that America should value the lives of young, healthy people more than those of old, sick individuals as they work to ram the health care plan through.. One such advisor, Dr. Ezekiel Emanuel, brother of Obama's chief of staff Rahm Emanuel, wrote in *The Lancet* in 2008: "Unlike allocation by sex or views of race, allocation by age is not invidious discrimination." We were all young once, the argument goes, and so denying the elderly and weak in order to care for the young and fit is just.

Our misguided nation is seriously misinformed with reference to the biblical view of life. There are those who believe in the *teleological* view of life. That view sees life as a means toward an end, not as an end in itself. Then there is the biblical view, or the *spiritualistic* view. The biblical view sets life apart as sacred because it is the creation and gift of God, and worthy within itself. Being divine, life needs no utilitarian or teleological function outside itself. Life is from God, and to God, and for God. We literally do not own our life or that of anyone else.

In contrast with that view, the liberal, secular view sees life as worthy only if it is productive in the sense that liberals define productivity: achievement, pleasure, activity and relationships (you can read that, for some, as meaning promiscuous sexual activity between any two people who want immediate gratification).

It does not take great imagination to see that this right to die will soon become the "requirement" to die. Wesley Smith, an expert on the culture of death, observes: "Now, a new medical hegemony is arising, one that proclaims the right to declare which of us have lives worth living and are therefore worth treating medically, and which of us do not. Unless people object strongly...to this duty to die...and legislatures take active steps to intervene, this new and deadly game of 'Doctor Knows Best' will be coming soon to a hospital near you."[1]

THE BATTLE FOR OUR VERY LIVES

We heard a lot about the cost of the Obama-Kennedy-Pelosi health care in mid-2009, but what should really have concerned us was its callousness. Among its many "provisions," meant to convey the idea that these are good things, will be the Government's provision of end-of-life resources. The bill would reduce physician services for Medicaid, for Seniors, and the poor. Advanced Care Planning will be used to dictate treatment as a patient's health deteriorates, and the Government will decide what level of treatments you can have. Senior citizens won't matter; after all, the Government doesn't have to pay Social Security to dead people.

The Obama Health Care Plan equals death. When government bureaucrats start calling the shots and they tell providers exactly what they can and cannot do — what they, the government, says will be paid — then Obama's takeover of health care will show that it is, in fact, a power grab. For Obama and other Statists, fetuses and dead seniors impose no additional health costs.

Contrary to the promises of politicians and lobbyists, new euthanasia laws are already being routinely abused in states like Oregon, resulting in the deaths of innocent Americans who were given no choice in the decision to end their lives. As more and more states pass legislation allowing euthanasia, and the sanctity of life is eroded further by a callous disregard for the lives of the weak and frail in our communities, it seems inevitable that national politics will meet the culture of death in a tragic uniting of forces determined to use health care costs, class warfare, and the plight of the sick, dying and the aged, to force euthanasia on all of us.

THE "SLIPPERY SLOPE"

Godless liberals mock the idea of a "slippery slope." In order to advance their agenda of death, they ridicule the notion that once you start to devalue life, there is no end in sight. They should study a group with whom they think they have no identity — the Nazis. The Third Reich began with eugenics, cleansing their race of those mentally challenged and deformed, and there is a direct line from eliminating those challenged people to the roaring ovens of Dachau, Buchenwald and Auschwitz. The Neo-Nazis are those pull-the-tube liberals. They are traveling down the same road as the lemmings that followed Hitler into the inferno of the Holocaust.

Stop considering the face of Terri Schiavo for a second, and picture your own mother or grandmother in the ICU of a city hospital. There she is in desperate need of immediate care. A doctor emerges representing the Quality of Life Assessment Team. He looks at your mother, perhaps the victim of a stroke and in an indeterminate medical condition. He determines that her quality of life may not live up to his elitist standards of human existence. Perhaps she will not be able to play golf at the country club, or participate in a bridge party, or take a flight to the Caribbean. She may only moan and drool in a rest home. Presto. His assessment of her quality of life is sufficient to withhold medical care from her, even against hers, or your wishes. And what is more, if the medical establishment decides she should die, he will have you arrested for giving her a drink of water.

Many would, and have objected that such accusations are nothing more than the Orwellian ravings of conspiracy theorists. If you are one who thinks so, consider this. On Good Friday 2005 Gabriel Keys took Terri Schiavo a cup of water as she was dying of dehydration in Woodside Hospice. Gabriel brought water to someone dying of thirst; a federal judge had demanded that she die of dehydration and starvation. As a ten-year-old, he is probably not conversant with this new morality requiring death. Gabriel was arrested, handcuffed, and taken away. Obviously, he took Jesus too seriously in the Lord's command that we give someone a cup of cold water. You can mark it down. As a result of what someone has called the "Twenty-first Century Scopes Trial," we will watch our own loved ones judicially murdered in the years ahead, if we do not act now. It is no exaggeration to say that the Obama Health Care Plan equals death.

Gene Tipps of Seymour, Texas, probably has a different view of the Schiavo case than many Americans. Gene was twenty in 1967 when a friend rolled the vehicle they were riding in, and Gene was injured. He was in a coma for eight years. During that time he needed gallbladder surgery that was performed regardless of his condition, saving his life. After undergoing the surgery he suddenly woke and started to chatter like a magpie. He could not talk enough to his astonished mother Gladys, who had never given up on him. Today Gene takes care of his aged mother and helps humanity by delivering meals to the elderly shut-ins of his community. If the godless pull-the-tube liberals had gotten their hands on him, he would be in his grave today. Instead, reporters from all over the world came to interview him after his miraculous Awakening, and he went on to graduate from college and enjoy a life that Barney Frank and his ilk would have stolen from him, if given the chance.

Consider, also, a thirty-year-old woman named Tracy Gaskill. Tracy was in an accident in 2002, and remained in a comatose state that required her to be nourished through a tube, much like Terri Schiavo's, for two- and a-half years. In 2005 she gradually began using her long-dormant throat muscles again. She laughed, she hummed, and she sipped water. Today, Tracy can talk. She began only with one word responses, but they were words that brought tears of joy to her grandparent's eyes. And, she can eat. If she could, Tracy says she would spend her day eating strawberry swirled ice cream and juicy watermelons and vanilla milkshakes from Sonic. What if the "death with dignity" crowd had decided after two years that Tracy no longer derived any enjoyment out of life, and therefore deserved to starve to death to prevent her from being a burden on her family?

Remember the story of Donald Herbert, age forty-three. Injured as a firefighter in 1995, he remained in a comatose condition for ten years. In April of 2005 he woke up and talked for fourteen hours straight, to the astonishment of everyone present.

Or, consider Kelly Ann Barker, thirty-five. She was diagnosed as being in a persistent vegetative state after being hit by an automobile in September, 2003. While an aunt was visiting her at Thanksgiving that year, Tracy suddenly slid her legs off the bed. The same doctors, who had pronounced her vegetative state to be irreversible, can't explain her sudden recovery. By 2006 she was sitting up, speaking with her family, and doing well in therapy.

None of these people would be alive today if the misguided liberals could have pulled the tube. Had they found them in time, they would have clambered up the steps of the Supreme Court themselves to plead for the order to starve these "burdens on society" to death. And the people who would have murdered them are waiting for your grandmother and even possibly for you, sanctimoniously justifying their actions as a method of population control for a sustainable world.

POPULATION CONTROL AND THE DEATH CULT

At the turn of the century, euthanasia and abortion are two of the methods of extermination now being used by those who believe the planet is overpopulated and our rate of growth is not sustainable. For people like Obama, the fifty million-and-counting abortions since Roe v. Wade means there are fifty million fewer people feeding at the trough. There is a growing movement that sees population control as an urgent necessity, if we are to survive and save the planet from dying. The supposed need to control the size of the population on Earth was one of many reasons offered in support of the Eugenics movement, so, naturally, the term population control became popular in politics and society alongside the Eugenics movement, and the environmental movement. It was spurred on by a marked decline in the death rate due to improved sanitation, housing, and nutrition. In response to growing populations, and the resulting societal and environmental problems attributed to that growth, as well as the additional human development that is inevitable in areas of growth, population control was proposed as a means of saving the planet from rising numbers of the earth's most destructive and abusive creatures — the humans.

In the early 1900s, different groups promoted different methods of reducing the population, but the most commonly supported topics were abortion, contraception, sterilization, Eugenics, and, yes, even simply eliminating entire groups of people. The population control movement has been greatly aided by the alarmist environmental movement, whose cries of global warming, and the eminent human destruction of the rainforest, a problem that is now reversing itself[2], led many in America to believe that humans were a plague on planet Earth. Over time, through media coverage and public school indoctrination, many American's wealth and successes were really excesses that would lead to poverty and death as Earth's resources dwindled.

Overseas, the extreme poverty in Third World countries was used by population control advocates as an example of what happens when there are more people to feed than there are resources. Of course, Africa's many natural resources, which are not tapped because dictatorial regimes prefer to keep people poor and dependent, were not included in the equation. If people are starving, it must be because the evil West is producing too many babies, and gobbling up the natural resources.

In the sixties a group of European industrialists called the Club of Rome produced a study that, using bad science, claimed the American standard of living was the cause of poverty and starvation on the other side of the planet, in poor and underdeveloped countries. Naturally, the warning that there were too many American babies being born was music to the death cult's ears. This alarmist view, which states that success in one country breeds death and destruction around the world, fed the arguments of socialists', globalists', and eugenicists' alike. In many circles, the HIV virus was even seen as a great benefit to humanity, rather than the devastatingly tragic cause of millions of deaths, especially in Africa.[3] In the process of turning population growth into a crisis, the death cult's target population grew to include not only the poor, unfit, and "useless eaters," but the rich and middle class, as well, for their evil excesses and abuse of the planet.

But America has its elitists too who, in a May 5, 2009 meeting in Manhattan, came to a general agreement that population control should be a major priority. And who are these world's elite billionaires giving to themselves the right to make overpopulation a top priority for their philanthropic endeavors? According to *The Times* it was convened by Microsoft mogul Bill Gates, and included David Rockefeller Jr., the patriarch of America's wealthiest dynasty, Warren Buffett and George Soros, financiers, Michael Bloomberg, the major of New York, and the media moguls Ted Turner and Oprah Winfrey.

Even as this book is being written, the News Watch services on the Internet, inform readers that the environmentalists are now pushing for a two child limit and abortion to save the environment. Never mind that, while ostensibly saving the environment, they are advocating a form of murder in order to eliminate babies. This comes from the U.K.'s government's Sustainable Government Commission, and from Jonathan Perritt, who chairs the commission and says, "I am unapologetic about asking people to connect up their own responsibility for their total environmental footprint and how they decide to procreate and how many children they think are appropriate."

The "Carbon Footprint"

There you have it…many of us have probably heard someone talk about the risk to our environment in terms of each person's "carbon footprint". It's become a common term used to describe the amount of resources each person consumes, as well as the damage their lifestyle does to the environment over the span of their lifetimes. While the term was coined in recent years, the idea behind it has been around for over a century.[4]

All of these environmental catch phrases and labels are designed to create fear and convince us that we must blame humanity, and especially Americans, for every problem that arises on our planet. In this twenty-first century world, the weather is no longer a natural phenomenon, but is caused by global warming. Disasters are also no longer natural because humans must have done something to disrupt the environment's natural balance, and the Earth's resources are no longer capable of sustaining human life without the help of an army of environmental activists. According to the United Nations and the many leaders who have bought into the environmental movement's warnings, population growth must be slowed to a "zero growth" level, or the earth will suffer life-ending harm. By convincing the masses that this threat is real and immanent, they know that many people will agree to go along with the death cult's agenda, if for no other reason than fear and a sense of self preservation for themselves and their families.

They have succeeded in instilling in each generation an increasing level of guilt for our environmental abuses. Add to that the devaluation of human life, class warfare that pits the haves against the have-nots, and the vilification of the disabled and elderly as burdens on society and the source of rising health care costs, and you have a recipe for mass murder in the name of political correctness.

If you think it is overreaching to say that this indoctrination of the masses will lead to millions upon millions of innocent victims being put to death, remember Terri Schiavo, and those like her, and consider the states that have recently passed laws legalizing euthanasia. Remember the fifty million babies that have been aborted in this country since Roe v. Wade. And, if that doesn't convince you of the death cult's willingness to control every aspect of our lives, consider the February, 2009 article in the UK's *Sunday Times* previously referred to. It bears emphasis. The chair of this commission, said, "Political leaders should stop dodging the issue of environmental harm caused by an expanding population." In other words, he wants people to stop being afraid to connect the dots and get on with presenting their final solution for the planet. He admonishes people to begin thinking about "how many children are appropriate" for a family. It seems Mr. Perritt thinks we are "working our way toward a position that says that having more than two children is irresponsible."

There you have it. We're in crisis mode and the planet must be saved, therefore Chinese style population control, where families are limited to only two children must be enforced globally. If you were wondering how Perritt's wife feels about this, I'm sure she is fine with his solution. Perritt has — you guessed it — two children, and plans to have no more. How convenient that two is the magic number that will save the planet.[5]

If our governments, even in free democratic countries like Britain, believe they should dictate to people how many children they are allowed to have, why should we doubt that they will also tell us when we need to be sterilized to prevent having any more babies, or when we should die so that our carbon footprint doesn't rise to an unsustainable level, or our medical bills don't unfairly burden others.

In different ways mandated "end of life care" is already being forced on us in America through right to die legislation, and the slow acceptance of euthanasia as an acceptable way to end a life. It's not hard to see how the Antichrist will be able to create his system of marking those loyal to him, and exterminating those who are not. Not only will the population be amazed at the miraculous signs and wonders he will demonstrate, and deify him, but they will have been desensitized to death by the common use of euthanasia, the use of abortion as birth control, and a global effort to deal with a plague of humans that are killing the planet by overpopulating it. In every way possible human life has been devalued so as to become expendable, and all for the good of a big rock hurtling through space in orbit around the sun. Millions will die because death became our friend, rather than the enemy God tells us it is. Yet, even in such evil times, there is hope in Christ.

HOPE!

Jesus Christ is the Lord of life. Wherever He is, there is hope. Those who do not know Him live in the sickness of despair. The nineteenth century Danish philosopher Soren Kierkegaard called despair the only "sickness unto death." By that, the great Christian existentialist described the very root of the culture of death. The culture of death does not recognize the Lord of Life. Because of that, they see only death, despair and the dolorous dirge of meaningless existence, punctuated by an intermittent moment of sensual pleasure before the light of life goes out. They would have possibly pulled the tube on Fanny J. Crosby, too. Blinded from birth, she sat in a room and wrote "Blessed Assurance" and "To God Be the Glory," hymns sung by millions all over the world every Sunday. They would have concluded that she had no quality of life, could not contribute to society, and should be eliminated.

The Lord of Life always holds out the promise of life. Where He is the Living Bread, we cannot withhold nourishment. Where He is the Living Water, we cannot withhold water. Where He is the Light of Life, we cannot turn out the lights and pull the plug that sustains life. Where He is the Good Shepherd, we cannot let godless liberals kill His sheep. Where He is the Door of the Sheepfold, we cannot bar the door of medical help to anyone. Where He is the Resurrection and the Life, we cannot despair of life for anyone, but must celebrate each life as a precious gift from God that none of us have the right to cut short. Will the scale tip? We can still make a difference!

CHAPTER EIGHT

Out of the Closet: Collision with the Culture

Thirty years ago no one questioned the idea that the traditional family was the cornerstone of American society and essential to its very survival...A "family" thirty years ago meant Mom, Dad, the kids — and on holidays, Grandpa, Grandma, aunts, cousins, and in-laws.

Congressman Wm. Dannemeyer in *Shadow in the Land*
(Published in 1989, an incredibly accurate foretelling
of what might happen if the then-rising homosexual
movement achieved its goals.)

Unlike the banning of prayer, Roe v Wade and the ongoing abortion issues, and most other defining moments in America's recent history, the virtual attack on society's long-held disgust with sexual perversion just seemed to happen. One night Americans went to bed with no question in their minds as to the definition of marriage and awoke finding themselves having to debate and defend marriage, this most basic of life's joys. The traditional family, indeed, this cornerstone of American society, came under attack. But did it really happen that quickly or has there been an organized agenda that has altered the way we view sexuality in America?

WHAT HAPPENED? WHERE DID NORMALCY GO?

Allow me a brief blast to the past for a reminder of key events which impacted and shaped our society today. Hear me; listen, because this definitely has collided with our culture and what's happened in America.

In the years leading up to World War II Americans were largely people living on farms or in small rural communities. Don't misunderstand, we had our great cities, New York, Chicago, Philadelphia and San Francisco, but the majority of our population still awoke to the sound of a rooster crowing or a cow mooing. People met and married neighbors and, for the most part, settled down near their families and built their lives. Men worked and women stayed at home and raised the children. I realize that the so-called liberated woman of today recoils at the very mention of that previous role, but that is the way it was. That was living a life of normalcy that had existed from time immemorial. The result of this was that men were mostly mixing with other men all day and the same was true for women with other women. Adultery, while it did happen, was rare due to the lack of anonymity, the close proximity of available partners and the shame factor. In addition, there were no television programs airing an endless dribbling of housewife unhappiness. In fact, there was no television and divorce was a dirty word.

People worked hard, tried to save their money, listened to the radio briefly in the evenings, children did their lessons, and they played games and read together. There was a lot of family togetherness. For a fortunate few there were silent movies presented in black and white. Westerns and slapstick comedy were the order of the day. The workweek was six days and on Sunday they went to church. Then, on Monday they did it all over again!

There were some holidays that were actually observed in a display of patriotism — flags were proudly flown and no one would have dared to desecrate the American flag. Americans stood up, took off their hats or caps, stood at attention and got a lump in their throats when they heard the National Anthem. This undoubtedly sounds very boring to the younger generation of today who cannot fathom a single moment of absolute silence even while attempting to sleep, but that is the way it was. One of the most anticipated holidays was Memorial Day — the day to honor veterans — and always it was on May 31, regardless if it came in the middle of the week! There would be a parade of locals, the WWI and II vets proudly marching, the high school band playing, the American flag carried by another local proudly leading the parade. At the cemetery there would be solemn words remembering the fallen servicemen, we would salute the flag, and then big guns were fired. Talk about nostalgia and patriotism. Some of us grew up in that kind of climate.

Marriage was between a man and a woman. The husband was the provider and head of the home. The wife was the heart of the home. Children obeyed their parents and all believed there was a God in heaven and that one day there would be judgment. Sounds simple, and compared to life today, it was.

California Congressman Dannemeyer, quoted at the outset of this chapter, in speaking of the "traditional family," and the way things were twenty or more years ago, at the time his book was published, said that there may have been some who would argue that people were narrow-minded then, but he didn't really think they were. "I believe they simply saw more clearly the importance of traditional family life to the survival of society as a whole. They recognized that promiscuous conduct threatened the very existence of family life...." It is an indisputable fact that the homosexual life-style is incapable of reproduction and doomed to certain extinction. In a very real sense, it is not a life-style but a "death-style."

BUT BACK THEN...NOW MORE THAN SIXTY YEARS LATER...

In the early morning hours of December 7, 1941 the Japanese unleashed the single most devastating event in America's history and thousands of Americans died in a matter of minutes. As America rallied, the boys came off the farm and out of the factories. They became sailors, marines, soldiers, airmen — service men and women — going off to defend our freedom. Many women left the home to fill the vacuum created by the departure of our men. Letters started arriving; now many of our loved ones were on foreign soil. And then the service flags started appearing in windows across the country — and when the gold stars appeared, we knew someone had lost a loved one, a husband, a father, a son, a daughter — the ultimate price had been paid for our freedom. America toiled for four years embroiled in a war on two fronts and life in America was changed forever. The war ended, some of our men never made it back home, others did but not necessarily to the farm, and the women stayed on their jobs. Men and women began working side by side and, as mainstream America became amenable to the idea that women can do more than just have and raise children and look after their families, America would never be the same!

THE SEXUAL REVOLUTION BEGINS

Then, television was born, more movie theaters began to dot our countryside, and in 1947, Alfred Kinsey founded his Institute for Research in Sex at Indiana University. For the first time Americans were challenged to talk openly about sex and sexual techniques. The taboos began to slowly ebb away. The closet door was open.

As America became enamored with the sexual revolution, adultery and its twin sister, divorce, began to skyrocket. Pornography began to permeate our society and with it came every kind of sexual perversion man could conjure up in his depraved mind. One of the latest perverse things to appear on the sexual scene is what young people call "Sexting," that is sending test messages of a sexual nature to each other. Some "experts" are defending it as a modern day "Spin the Bottle" game.

"Spin the Bottle," a long, long ago parlor game, was child's innocent play and, as compared to "Sexting," there just is no comparison. What an awful and incredible analogy! Mark R. Levin, nationally syndicated talk-radio host and best-selling author, stated that this is much more widespread than people think. "Sexting is extremely widespread and common." He maintains that if you asked a kid what percentage of her top ten friends are sex-texting, she'd say 100 percent.

Government abuse of parental rights was shown in a freshman class of kids as young as fourteen-years-old who were required to attend a "Gay Straight Alliance Network" panel discussion led by "gay" and "lesbian" upperclassmen. It wasn't enough that students at Deerfield High, in Deerfield, Illinois, were being exposed to improper and offensive material relative to unhealthy and high-risk homosexual behavior, but they were told by teachers to lie about this to their parents. Students had to sign a "confidentiality agreement" through which they promised not to tell anyone — including their own parents — about the seminar. This kind of situation is clearly beyond the pale!

But back to some of the history of this sexual revolution — Kinsey opened a door and then it happened! Homosexuality, which is one of the logical conclusions of a society in the bonds of porn, came out of the closet and into our homes via the movie theaters, then television, and yes, even the classroom and our churches. History is replete with cultures, civilizations and nations who have passed into the pages of history once they delved into the perverse.

One hardly knows where to begin in seeking to shed some light on how homosexuality came out of the closet to where it is today. Dannemeyer's summation of the history of the movement — and make no mistake, this is a well-orchestrated movement — brings it into focus showing, as he does, what their intent was then and how, through the years, it has been and is being accomplished. In fact, it's no stretch to say that the congressman was truly prophetic in what he said, wrote, and sought to do to warn the country and the Washington establishment then.[1]

As is known now, Gay and Lesbian Parades are a well-publicized yearly event nationwide with groups marching and participating that included, in 1988, Dykes and Tykes, Dignity (Catholic homosexuals), the Gay Men's Health Crisis, the National Gay and Lesbian Task Force, and NAMBLA (the North American Man-Boy Love Association (composed of pedophiles, more precisely, of men who like to have sex with very young boys), and others. In writing about this parade that took place in 1988, the congressman said: "In many respects the relatively high profile of NAMBLA defines the progress that homosexuals have made over the past thirty-five years. Had the existence of such a group been known in the 1950s, they would have been hounded out of town or thrown into jail, where they would have been lucky to survive their sentences, since even hardened convicts in earlier times had little patience with child molesters."[2] Now think about that, the year it was written, and what has happened in succeeding years. It is mind-boggling!

Using the rhetoric of the civil rights movement, they put out newsletters, hold conventions, and appear on network television talk shows. Little boys, they say, have as much right as adults to engage in consensual sex, and only a repressive society would prevent them from enjoying such exquisite pleasures at the earliest possible age.3

I point this out so you can see the ongoing progression of the homosexual movement which embraces and encourages organizations such as NAMBLA.

In fact, in June 2009, in a presidential proclamation on the White House website, Barak Obama lauded what he called "the determination and dedication" of the LGBT movement by proclaiming the month as "Lesbian, Gay, Bisexual, and Transgender Pride Month." Then, the president hosted a reception at the White House to celebrate the event. He had no time to host an event for the National Day of Prayer, nor did he have time to accept an invitation to convey greetings and a few remarks to the couple hundred thousand who came to Washington for their annual March for Life.

"A NATION SINKING TO ITS KNEES"

When a movement such as what homosexuals represent can march down our main thoroughfares, with official permission and protection of the police, and are constitutionally blessed they are a political force with a political agenda and, as Dannemeyer pointed out, they have brought us, as a "nation sinking to its knees." We have "surrendered to this growing army of revolutionaries without firing a shot, indeed, without more than a word or two of protest. The homosexual blitzkrieg has been better planned and better executed than Hitler's. Unlike the French, who wept in the streets of Paris as the Germans marched by, we don't even know we've been conquered — at least not yet."4

How has this happened? Homosexual activists first began to emerge from the shadows in the seventies, demanding their "rights," insisting they were the "victims of bigotry," demanding that they "not be discriminated against because of an accident of birth." In order to accommodate their demands, we would have to discard those unquestioned values that have always undergirded the American social order. Homosexuals began to publicly proclaim pride in their deviant behavior. They organized clubs and sought to make inroads into college campuses and schools. They compared themselves to women and Blacks claiming civil rights; and by the late 1970s they were demanding that they be allowed to lead their own lives without interference from government. Homosexuals were demanding that sodomy laws be abolished, and that their "life-styles" be recognized as a permissible alternative to more traditional arrangements. Everybody was suddenly out of the closet, homosexual was "in", and a small but substantial homosexual industry began to flourish.

American "liberals" and "moderates" began to cave in. Such "liberals," ardent in support of the civil rights movement and the women's movement, were distressed at the idea of "gay bashing" and began to consider endorsing legislation to prohibit the firing of homosexuals because of their sexual habits.

Among those "liberals" and "moderates" were some of the most influential people in the nation: editors and staff members of such major newspapers as the *New York Times, The Washington Post,* and the *Los Angeles Times*; reporters and producers of news programs on the major networks; columnists and contributors; and the leading academic minds of the Left. One of the main supporters of this perversion was none other than the late Teddy Kennedy! The leaders of the homosexual movement knew they would have to bring most of the doubters into the fold before they could achieve the kind of results that Blacks and feminists had achieved. So what did they do? How were they to achieve that?

HOMOSEXUALS ON THE THRESHOLD OF A NEW EXISTENCE AND THE TRANSFORMATION OF THEIR RHETORIC

Progress was being made; homosexuals saw themselves on the threshold of a new existence, and they knew they needed different words to define the new status they were achieving. Congressman Dannemeyer, to his eternal credit, laid all of this out brilliantly in the aforementioned book,

Shadow in the Land. And what a large shadow they began to cast! As he said, "Adam had named all the creatures in Eden. In the America of the late twentieth century, the homosexual was the New Adam."

They had to replace objectionable terms with more positive terms, words that would carry highly pleasant and seductive connotations. Once such a word was in place, they could use it to attract people to their cause. So what do you suppose they chose? How about the word *gay*? It was being used in France to describe homosexuals. The word means "happy and carefree." Yeh, let's go for it! So men and women stopped being "homosexual" and started being "gay" and the effect on the public was incredibly good! Now they weren't being defined by their sexual habits but they were being presented as having a certain lighthearted happiness about them that others by implication lacked.

Once the word *gay* became a part of the official homosexual lexicon, and imposing it on the nation's reluctant majority, homosexuals cast around for a word to designate their enemies — that is, the "straight" community, in particular those who opposed the toleration of homosexual practices. Now guess what the word was that they decided upon? Have you or someone you know ever been called a *homophobe,* or *homophobic?* So now those who disapprove of the practices of homosexuals are the ones who are mentally unbalanced, they are in the grips of a "phobia" — clearly an abnormal condition. Excuse me…

So whether the majority of citizens who disapprove of homosexual practices realize it or not, at this point it doesn't really matter because these terms have become acceptable terms in public and political discourse and have had a profound effect on the dialogue concerning crucial issues.

There are many other such terms that have come into existence, but I'll only focus on the phrases *"sexual orientation,"* formerly *"sexual preference."* Preference implies choice, and the line of argument that has proven the most successful is that homosexuality is inherited, that it is the result of genetic or hormonal factors that were beyond the control of the individual, thus they are "oriented" that way, that it is "natural" and "normal" for them, they are "born that way." Never mind that a substantial body of medical and psychological opinion disproving this has been shown. Another rhetorical shift was needed; sexuality couldn't be a "preference." Homosexuality did not come from the womb. You will never find God creating or championing the unnatural, and homosexuality is against nature.

The Bible says, "You shall not lie with a male as with a woman; it is an abomination" (Lev. 18:22)? And there are *many* other such verses discussed in other places in the Bible. Every single one of them condemns homosexual conduct in unqualified terms; there is no scriptural text, anywhere that approves of it. This is depravity! God hates it! He didn't cause it. The Bible says nothing about homosexual *orientation*; its restraints apply to behavior. How could a loving and just God declare this to be an abomination if He created it? No way! (See Appendix 5 for biblical texts on homosexuality.)

AND THEN THERE WAS ANITA BRYANT...

Remember Anita Bryant, the name synonymous with her trademark rendition of "Battle Hymn of the Republic," the woman whom the Florida Citrus Commission named their spokeswoman, who was called the Sunshine-Tree Girl? There will be many who recall the name Anita Bryant in connection with the Bob Hope Holiday Tours, and the seven years that she accompanied Hope's troupe singing to the live audiences of responsive servicemen, and how they loved her in the Caribbean, the Arctic, the Pacific, and the Far East. Anita never forgot, nor did the GIs who were in Vietnam, the night she sang "Silent Night" while lethal red-tracer bullets whined and heavy explosions rocked the area. Hope's troupe went to the front lines, where other visitors seldom ventured. What a group they were exemplifying everything good about America!

A beautiful young woman, Anita had become Miss Oklahoma and then on to the neon-glistening boardwalk of Atlantic City where she became the second runner-up to Miss America. In her journey Anita never abandoned her belief in God, the Bible, and Jesus Christ as her personal Savior. She was down-to-earth, real, believable, and a woman of faith. She also married and began raising a family.

But there is something else for which this woman needs to be remembered. In January 1977, Anita and her husband Bob, along with fifty other Miami citizens, stepped out in opposition to a proposed ordinance that, among other things, would allow known practicing homosexuals to teach in private and religious schools. Hold on! Bob and Anita had children in this school district. In stepping out, they became involved in a dramatic and emotional struggle with militant homosexuals. Immediately the dispute erupted into a full-blown national issue. The news media seized the opportunity. In *Time* and *Newsweek,* in television and radio reports, and in major newspaper headlines across the nation the story broke and expanded from a referendum campaign into a multitude of complex social issues. It was a controversy that wouldn't go away, a Mother standing up because she was concerned about her children, and other parents' children.

I am telling you Anita's story because it dramatically shows how the homosexuals' agenda was playing itself out at that crucial time in their history of demanding their so-called "rights." *The Anita Bryant Story* was published that same year. In it she spoke the truth in a compelling way. A reporter had noted that Anita had never been known before to raise her voice in anything but song. And he was right. But she said, "God put a flame in my heart, and I've learned to obey God regardless of the circumstances."

The consequences were incredible. Anita stuck by her biblical convictions and what the Bible said. Seldom in twentieth-century history has one person been subjected to the kind of attack Anita Bryant endured. Boycotts of products for which she was the spokesperson threatened their livelihood, and in the end, she lost her contracts. Bumper stickers and T-shirts assailed her. Protest marches and demonstrations involving hundreds of thousands were staged from coast to coast. She was the butt of jokes on radio and TV. She and her family received death threats, prank phone calls, bomb scares, and hate mail. More than one newspaper said she was the kicking object for the hysterical. While an amazing and encouraging groundswell of support for Anita grew throughout the country, the media, for the most part, chose to support the homosexual community. Through it all, the Lord sustained Anita, Bob, and their children. That story was told in Bob and Anita's book *At Any Cost* (1978).

Anita Bryant was a phenomenon of the late seventies — an entertainer who was willing to stand up to the vilest and most scurrilous public abuse for the sake of morality, simple decency, and the Word of God. She suffered much. She paid a tremendous price. But her confidence always rested in God. The Tulsa, Oklahoma, *Tribune*, described her as a square gal out of Tulsa originally, "who believes in such things as blueberry and apple pie, God, country and the difference between men and women." Anita liked that. She will always be remembered as a witness to and defender of the truth in the twentieth century. And for that, she received the honor of being included in the book *100 Christian Women Who Changed the 20th Century.*5

THE NEW SEX EDUCATION IN SCHOOLS AND AIDS "EDUCATION"

For many years the homosexual organizations made minimal headway against people with good sense, like the Anita Bryant's of the nation. But time has now revealed what the homosexual movement has achieved in getting more explicit and extensive sex education classes in our schools, as a means of introducing students, as young as those in fifth grade, to the practices of homosexuality. Then in one of the great and tragic ironies of our time, AIDS — a direct result of the sexual revolution and its rampant homosexual behavior — gave the sex educators the very opportunity they needed to ram through mandatory programs.

Organizations like Planned Parenthood and the Sex Information and Education Council of the United States (SIECUS) used statistics and information geared to their points of view, to argue in favor of more sex education for all young Americans. To "avoid bigotry" the public schools were enjoined to teach heterosexuality and homosexuality without bias. Panicked by predictions of an "explosion" of AIDS into the heterosexual community and ignorant of the demonstrable failure of such education classes in preventing pregnancy, school officials all over the country bit the bullet and adopted emergency measures, in many cases despite the moral reservations they held personally.6

Before leaving the subject of what is taking place in some of the schools across the nation, I want to tell you what happened in a school in northern California as told to me by a grandmother friend. "A few years ago when two of my granddaughters were still in public school my daughter felt compelled to remove them from that environment. My daughter called and asked me to pray specifically while she went to the school to talk to the principal. My granddaughter Christa was being threatened by a couple of girls. She had seen them kissing and making out. One of these girls brought a knife in her backpack, found my granddaughter the next day, and, brandishing the knife in Christa's face, menaced her saying they'd get her if she reported on them. My granddaughter immediately called her parents and they came to the school and got both of their daughters. They asked the principal to take action, but he said he was powerless to do that. My daughter and son-in-law were left with only one option — they had to remove their daughters from the school and enroll them elsewhere."

Perhaps you are thinking, "Oh, but that couldn't happen in the United States…" Think again. It did happen, and things similar to that have been happening for years now. Forces have been at work for decades organized in ways so as to alter our society. There are programs in schools throughout the nation that openly promote homosexuality and condemn anyone who believes that such deviant behavior is abnormal or undesirable. Try to stand up to it or bring about change and you are labeled…what? Yes, you learned the word: *homophobic!*

INTERNET HEADLINE NEWS

Even as this book is being finalized, Internet news headlines tell the distressing, disturbing story. Just a casual look, bears this out:

- **Gay issues may splinter churches this summer**
- **Why are 'Conservative' Leaders Selling Out on 'Civil Unions'?**

- Church of Scotland upholds gay minister's appointment
- 'Gay' pundit says 'hate crimes' a scam
- Gay-on-Gay 'hate crimes'
- Research: 'Hate crimes' prelude to incest, polygamy
- Government to force gay youth workers on church
- District gags 14-year-olds after 'gay' indoctrination
- Christian Clergy Rally on Opposite Sides of Gay Marriage Debate

PERVERSION OF SEX IS BIBLICALLY PROHIBITED

The Bible is absolutely clear about its prohibitions with regard to perversions of sex; anyone who says otherwise simply does not know the Word of God. "Our religious traditions and scriptures teach us that wherever love is present, God is also present," so goes the reasoning and rationale for abominable practices that some in the clergy and churches are now supporting.[1] "We declare that our faith calls us to affirm marriage equality for loving, same-sex couples," said the Rev. Dennis Wiley, pastor of Covenant Baptist Church, at a gathering..., according to *The Washington Post*. "We affirm the right of loving same-gender couples to enter into such relationships on an equal basis with loving heterosexual couples," the coalition, called D. C. Clergy United for Marriage and Equality, comprised of more than 100 clergy from various faiths, launched this declaration, affirming same-sex marriages as "holy and good."[7]

In stark contrast, conservative clergy have made public cries, committing themselves to fight any attempts to redefine marriage. The Stand 4 Marriage D. C. clergy believe homosexual behavior is not in line with Scripture. (Once again, I refer you to Appendix 5 where the scriptural injunctions against perverted sex are provided.) One of the things this D.C. clergy group pointed out in a letter to its mayor and the city council was that same-sex marriage proponents' claim that marriage is an issue of civil rights, was offensive to them, that is "to those of us who have been standing up for true civil rights all our lives."[8]

They went on to explain: "Racial discrimination has always been not only wrong, but irrational, because race is a characteristic which is inborn, involuntary, immutable, innocuous, and in the Constitution. None of these criteria apply to the choice to engage in homosexual relationships," they stated.[2]

This is a battle that isn't over as more states debate same-sex marriage bills. Gay and lesbian couples across the country have filed lawsuits challenging the constitutionality of the federal Defense of Marriage Act, and in California Proposition 8 where the State Supreme Court upheld a constitutional amendment banning same-sex marriage. That said, trust me this victory is temporary. Four states have already crossed the line including Massachusetts and Vermont. By the way, for same-sex couples fussing over what to serve at their wedding reception, Ben & Jerry's has a new dessert course suggestion: How about Hubby Hubby ice cream? That's right, the premium ice cream maker, renowned for its publicity stunts, has renamed its popular Chubby Hubby flavor to recognize the fact that Vermont's decision to grant gays and lesbians the right to marry took effect on Tuesday, September 2, 2009.

The proponents of gay marriage are well organized, well funded and will not tolerate any form of opposition. Mark my word; they will use violence if necessary to have their way. The result will be more and more states will cave to this pressure to be tolerant and in the end the perverse will win.

Moral Apathy

One result of the moral apathy that has engulfed our country is the pervasive presence of pornography in all areas of our culture. Pornography has spread like a plague across the Internet, becoming nearly unavoidable if one spends any amount of time surfing websites. Sexual addiction has become a common problem for many men, and to a lesser degree, women, even among those who call themselves Christians. Very real damage has been inflicted on individuals, families and marriages. Our lack of respect for life has had an effect on our respect for each other, and for the Christian values and morals that set us apart from many other countries. Women have become mere objects in a parade of lust, sex, and debauchery that is splashed across our TV screens, our city streets, billboards, and in our magazines. Any mention of abstinence or modesty is mocked. Indeed, America is at yet another tipping point.

CHAPTER NINE

The War on Christianity

> *In Germany they came first for the Communists, and I didn't speak up because I wasn't a Communist. Then they came for the Jews, and I didn't speak up because I wasn't a Jew. Then they came for the trade unionists, and I didn't speak up because I wasn't a trade unionist. Then they came for the Catholics, and I didn't speak up because I was a Protestant. Then they came for me, and by that time no one was left to speak up.*

Martin Niemoller
(Pastor of a Confessing Church in Berlin who was sentenced to the Sachsenhausen Concentration Camp by Hitler himself)

There is a war being fought each moment of the day in our country. This war is not the war on terrorism and the battleground is not Iraq, nor is it Afghanistan. Just as the first shot of America's Revolutionary War was fired at Concord and came to be known as, "the shot heard around the world". Just such a shot was fired in this war, only it was not from a musket in a field but rather from the mouth of an attorney in a courtroom. The warriors were identified. The American Civil Liberties Union (the ACLU) declared open war on Christianity. This shot was fired in 1917 when the National Civil Liberties Bureau became the ACLU in 1920. It was a good idea gone awry. In the beginning the organization sought to protect America's freedoms from government bullying. Sadly, as is often the case, good ideas become corrupted over time. Fast forward eighty plus years and we have an organization that now fights to rid these United States from any expression of Christianity and who spends untold millions of dollars in frivolous lawsuits and threats against anyone who dares name the name of Jesus Christ in the marketplace.

Isn't it somewhat ironic that the Congress of the United States opens their sessions with prayer? Isn't it odd that both The House and Senate have chaplains? Yet, we are not allowed to pray in the public schools of this land birthed for the purpose of freedom of religion. How did we get in this mess? This is America at yet another tipping point!

American history is vividly clear that faith in God and reverence for the Bible provided the basis for the founding of this nation. That same reverence by many of our presidents has had a profound impact on the greatness of our nation. Benjamin Hart, writing in *Faith and Freedom: The Christian Roots of American Liberty*, makes the chilling statement that one should consider liberty to be in grave danger if an American political leader were to announce that he had no religious convictions, or that he drew his morality from some other source than the Bible and the Judeo-Christian tradition. That is enough to make your hair stand on end when you consider where we are now in the first decade of the twenty-first century.

"A CULTURAL TSUNAMI"

The world in which we live is being called many things. Billy Graham has said, "We live in a time when the world is in turmoil. But not in my lifetime have I ever seen so many problems."

Dave Wilkerson (remember him and the book, *The Cross and the Switchblade?*), has a ministry in the heart of Times Square, New York, and he said in one of his newsletters, "We live in the most wicked time in history. Our present generation is many times worse than that of Nineveh or Sodom. We're more stiff-necked than ancient Israel, more violent than in Noah's day. If ever there was a time the world needed godly saints of intense faith, it's now." He called these times "a cultural tsunami."

Chuck Swindoll writes that we live in a corrupt, savage, hell-bent, degenerate world. Carl Henry writes of the twilight of our culture; Malcolm Muggeridge predicts the end of Christendom. Francis Schaeffer warns of the spiritual collapse of the West. C. S. Lewis, writing in *God in the Dock,* speaks of "bad rulers" as "fallen men, and, therefore, [being] neither very wise nor very good. As it is, they will usually be unbelievers. And since wisdom and virtue are not the only or the commonest qualifications for a place in the government, they will not often be even the best unbelievers."[i]

In book after book, in magazine articles — even secular journals such as *Newsweek* and *Time* decrying a "moral malaise overhanging American life" — in Internet blogs, reports, stories and articles, as Chuck Colson says reflecting on what's being written and said, "a crisis of immense proportions is upon us."

Amplifying on this "crisis," Colson explains: "[The crisis] is not from the threat of nuclear holocaust or a stock market collapse, not from the greenhouse effect or trade deficits, not from East-West relations or ferment in the Middle East. Though all these represent serious problems, in the end they will not be our undoing.

"No, the crisis that threatens us, the force that could topple our monuments and destroy our very foundation, is within ourselves. The crisis is in the character of our culture, where the values that restrain inner vices and develop inner virtues are eroding. Unprincipled men and women, disdainful of their moral heritage and skeptical of Truth itself, are destroying our civilization by weakening the very pillars upon which it rests....

"The crisis is not political; it is moral and spiritual. And so is the solution. That's why Christians are the only ones who can offer viable answers."[2]

To all of this, and much more that has been and continues to be said every day, I am in agreement. I see it as a war against Christianity. We are living in what is called a "postmodern" society — postmodern, post-Christian, post-everything-that-is-decent- America. Simply put, it's a slide from truth. The erosion of absolutes and truth is a major problem in our nation today. A friend describes this culture in which we live, as a four-letter world — a world that can be described with words like guns, kill, fear, poor, sick, worn, vile. And yes, our forty-third president, George W. Bush, had it right, there is another four-letter word, *evil.*

David Aikman in his book, *Great Souls,* speaks of this: "We are said to be living in a postmodern age, an epoch where ancient and long-held beliefs are not only no longer accepted by most people, they are not even considered worth holding up to the challenge of logical skepticism. People of the wretchedly named 'Generation X,' the children of the baby boomers, are themselves aging. Will they and those who follow them out into life confirm Friedrich Nietzsche's prediction of a century ago that, with God supposedly banished from men's discourse, human culture will become increasingly 'weightless'? It will be up to later generations, of course, to provide a definitive answer to that question."[3] Aikman was a former senior correspondent for *Time Magazine.*

"IN" BUT NOT "OF" THIS WORLD

The apostle Paul said that we are "in the world," but we are not to be "of the world." Most of us are familiar with that. We are to be identifiably Christian within our culture, not compromising nor conforming to it, and that produces an "in-the-world/not of-the-world tension." We are twice-born people living in the world of the once-born. Romans 8 talks about this speaking of being carnally minded and spiritually minded. Always, in age-appropriate ways, we will introduce biblical truths into our lifestyles and conversations, not something done in a pretentious, forced way, but this should be a naturally occurring outgrowth of our relationship with God. Because the Bible is forever relevant and includes moral absolutes — these unchanging principles defining right and wrong will be a distinct part of who we are.

In Luke 18:8 Jesus is talking to His disciples and He asks a question: "When I, the Messiah, return, how many will I find who have faith?" (*The Living Bible*)

The implication of that is plain. Faith can be lost in one generation. If parents, grandparents, and caregivers aren't passing on the baton of faith then it will be lost. And in the kind of world in which we now find ourselves living, that is happening. There are many forces vying for our time and attention, so many distractions and yes, so much opposition outright and some subtle — our schools, television, the Internet, friends, the world — the things talked about in previous chapters of this book.

"AS IN THE DAYS OF NOAH..."

Bible-reading Christians are familiar with Jesus' statement "Just as it was in the days of Noah, so also will it be in the days of the Son of Man. People were eating, drinking, marrying and being given in marriage up to the day Noah entered the ark. Then the flood came and destroyed them all" (Luke 17:26, 27 NIV). *The Living Bible* puts it like this: "[When I return] the world will be [as indifferent to the things of God] as the people were in Noah's day...just as usual..."

The indifference, the apathy, the disregard...yes, even the hatred, the outright scorn, the mocking, the total rejection...it's evident, all around us.

Nail-pounding Noah, quite possibly 120 years of working on that boat, no water in sight, not a lake, river, or even so much as a stream. No oceans. But Noah was doing what God had told him to do. How he must have faced the ridicule of his contemporaries! Can you imagine it? But oh, the faith that Noah had! Walking by faith is difficult because we're asked to believe what we can't see. Believing beyond the optic nerve — trusting beyond what is visible to the eye.

What do those without faith and trust in God do when faced with the unthinkables and the enormity of their situations?

What were those days like in which Noah lived? The generation of Noah lived as if God didn't exist. The Bible says that likewise, as it was in the days of Noah's nephew Lot, they drank, they bought, they sold, they planted, they built (vss. 28-29). Noah's generation, Lot's generation. The people around them just didn't get it, they had a sense of false security, unbelief and no faith characterized their lives. Does that sound like the world in which we live today?

Eugene Peterson in *The Message* says, "The time of the Son of Man will be just like the time of Noah — everyone carrying on as usual, having a good time right up to the day Noah boarded the ship. They suspected nothing until the flood hit and swept everything away.

"It was the same in the time of Lot — the people carrying on, having a good time, business as usual right up to the day Lot walked out of Sodom and a firestorm swept down and burned everything to a crisp. That's how it will be — sudden, total — when the Son of Man is revealed" (Luke 17:26-28).

THE CULTURE WARS

Yes, life as usual. Bill O'Reilly (Fox News Cable) said, "The culture war is getting bloodier. People better step up fast or the cultural war will be lost." He brilliantly presents the case in his book *Culture Warrior* where he talks about the armies of secularism rising and the public is largely unaware of what is taking place.

If you pay attention to the culture wars, it is clear who the shock troops are. The American Civil Liberties Union (ACLU) is the vanguard, waging a war of legal maneuvers designed to ensure secular policies without having to go to the ballot box, blitzing the legal system, promoting progressive causes and banishing traditional ones.[4]

In talking to Franklin Graham (Billy Graham's son), he and O'Reilly agreed that there is "a very intense spiritual war" going on.

Who is lining up in "battle formation" to do battle in this spiritual and cultural war? Networks control the slant of the news, and the anti-God ultra-liberal slant is relentless. The Internet smear merchants have joined forces with the mainline TV and print media and their ideological commitment to leftist views. These are the enablers for the frontline troops. Throw in the financing of the left-wing billionaires and the Hollywood elite and you have a mix ready, willing, and able to do battle, "guns" blazing, as it were, for the secular-progressive side.

Tragically — and that is the right word to use, no exaggeration — the "traditional army" is largely on leave. Many Americans are disengaged from this conflict, in fact, they aren't even aware it's under way. We are engaged in a war against Christianity. "Unless traditional Americans wake up and pay attention to important things like the culture war, they are going to arise some morning and find their old country has vanished…"⁵ Apathy, indifference, life as usual…

THE POWERFUL AND BATTLE-READY MEDIA BRIGADE

To their shame, while brave American military men and women were fighting valiantly in far-flung places, in the spring of 2009, the media was focused on celebrities rather than the shooting of a young recruit at a base in Texas. Further illustrating the influence of the powerful and battle-ready Media Brigade was Michael Jackson's June 25 death which overshadowed all other news for almost two weeks, and evening news programs, eleven days after his death, who dedicated less than one minute of combined airtime to the death of seven soldiers in Afghanistan while Jackson received nearly nineteen minutes of airtime. Networks overlooked topics that truly impact American families such as health care reform, North Korea's nuclear weapons and troop withdrawal from Iraq in favor of continued Jackson coverage. The overabundance of "news" about Michael Jackson clearly showed celebrity as the nation's top priority.

I think this says something about our culture, and I'm not intending to belabor the issue, but when the media continually painted Jackson as an innocent victim of circumstances, it overlooked facts — he was repeatedly accused of child molestation, and settled one suit out of court for $22 million; numerous friends, acquaintances and employees reported serious drug abuse (which may, in fact, have killed him); his multiple plastic surgeries and other strange appearance alterations amounted to what some called self-mutilation; despite vast intellectual and real property holdings and lucrative revenue streams, Jackson died $400 million in debt, owing to a decadent, sumptuous and irresponsible lifestyle that indulged every whim.⁶

Pervasive secular bias is rampant in America's print press and the TV media as well.

WE HAVE AN ADVERSARY

While there are many forces conspiring to overtake our country in subtle, and some-not-so subtle ways, there is one factor overriding all others which, when acknowledged and understood, can help us do personal battle on our own turf. We are told who this is and how to counterattack: "Be careful — watch out for attacks from Satan, your great enemy. He prowls around like a hungry, roaring lion, looking for some victim to tear apart. Stand firm when he attacks. Trust the Lord…" (1 Pet. 5:8 TLB).

This is a theme woven throughout the Bible. This enemy is clearly portrayed as an adversary. We are warned that we face the wrath of a raving-mad devil bent on devouring God's people (Rev. 12:12). Satan already has the world in his grasp, why waste time on them? His primary target is Christians, and he is blinding the eyes of all he possibly can. This is not hyperbole — extravagant exaggeration of any kind — the biblical pronouncements are warnings meant to help us understand the strategy of this enemy. We are advised to flee to escape the snares of the devil (2 Tim. 2:26). This is not cowardly fleeing, knowing when to run, to flee, is as important in spiritual battle as knowing when and how to fight what the Bible calls "the good fight of faith" (see 1 Tim. 6:11, 12).

THE ARMOR OF GOD

We are not powerless in this battle being waged against the forces of evil in the world. Ephesians 6:10-20 outlines the full armor of God so that we can take our stand against the devil's schemes. This isn't a struggle against flesh and blood, but it is against rulers and authorities, against the powers of this dark world and against the spiritual forces of evil, headed by Satan, who is a vicious fighter. Spiritual warfare is real; but we can be battle ready at all times.

Here are the pieces of armor, their use, and the application. The entire body needs to be armed, and as we fight in this battle, we can draw upon the strength and power God supplies:

● The belt of truth; the enemy fights with lies, and sometimes those lies sound like truth, but believers have God's truth, which can defeat Satan's lies.

● The breastplate of righteousness; Satan often attacks our hearts — the seat of our emotions, self-worth and trust. God's righteousness is the breastplate that protects our hearts and ensures his approval.

● Footgear for our feet enabling us to be ready to tell others that true peace is available in God — good news everyone needs to hear.

● The shield of faith is to protect us from the flaming arrows, as it were, of insults, setbacks, and temptations. With God's perspective, we can see beyond our circumstances and know that ultimate victory is ours.

● The helmet of salvation is to protect our minds from doubting what God will do for us and what he has already accomplished in Jesus.

● The sword of the Spirit and the Word of God, and it is the only weapon of offense in this list of armor. There are times when we need to take the offensive against Satan; we can do that as we trust in the truth of God's Word.

And then we are told to pray on all occasions, with all kinds of prayers and requests (vs. 18). How can we do this? Let your life be a prayer — quick, brief cries — your habitual response to every situation you confront throughout the day. A friend calls them "telegram prayers" — faster than the Internet. You don't have to isolate yourself from other people, nor do you have to drop to your knees, or clutch a rosary in your hands. You can make prayer your life and your life a prayer while living in a world that desperately needs God's powerful influence.[7]

REFLECTIONS OF THE LIGHT OF CHRIST

"We live in a culture that by all accounts is descending into darkness, and our job is to reflect the light of Christ,"[8] writes Mark Galli, senior managing editor of *Christianity Today.* That is a very thought-provoking statement.

As one thinks about living in this new Dark Age period and the many signs all about us which confirm this descent, I come back to what the Gospel of John tells us: "And this is the condemnation, that the light has come into the world, and men loved darkness rather than light, because their deeds were evil. For everyone practicing evil hates the light and does not come to the light, lest his deeds should be exposed. But he who does the truth comes to the light, that his deeds may be clearly seen, that they have been done in God" (John 3:19-21 NKJ).

How do we do battle in the war on Christianity? We reflect the light of Christ. Many don't want their lives exposed to God's light because they fear what will be revealed. The light in you might expose some of the darkness in their lives. They don't want that kind of change. Pray that they will come to see how much better it is to live in light than in darkness.

CHAPTER TEN

Welcome to Obamamerica

We live in a new dark age.

Charles Colson

in *Against the Night: Living in the New Dark Ages*[ii]

When principles that run against your deepest convictions begin to win the day, then battle is your calling, and peace has become sin; you must, at the price of dearest peace, lay your convictions bare before friend and enemy, with all the fire of your faith.

Abraham Kuyper

As quoted by Colson in the above book.[2]

With the inauguration of Barak Obama as the president of the United States in 2009, a new chapter in the history of this nation was begun. If the opening pages of that history are any indication of what may yet happen, our deepest convictions are being trampled upon, battle lines appear to be drawn, peace a thing of the past, the "barbarians" at the gate, and a deepening dark age encroaches. It *is* a nervous age.

A much-respected pastor-writer of the twentieth century was A. W. Tozer whose insights have an enduring quality about them and it was his statement that caught my attention: "*We who live in this nervous age would be wise to meditate on our lives and our days long and often before the face of God and on the edge of eternity. For we are made for eternity as* *certainly as we are made for time, and as responsible moral beings we must deal with both."*₃

Linked with the above statements, it becomes a call that impacts the mind with a powerful wallop. Colson states that in a few generations, or a few hundred years, and maybe our new dark age will dawn into a new morning. But the question is asked, "What about today?" Even as Colson wrote, and even now as I write, unjust laws are being written, political cowardice and greed mortgages our and our progenitor's futures, spending is out of control, and we cannot ignore immediate concerns like these. That's just a short list of concerns; the actual list is much longer and will continue to accelerate in the weeks and months ahead. Welcome to Obamamerica! Those concerns are major.

Colson quotes another fine author, Harry Blamires, who describes our dilemma well: "As a thinking being, the modern Christian has succumbed to secularization. He accepts religion — its morality, its worship, its spiritual culture, but he rejects the religious view of life, the view which sets all earthly issues within the context of the eternal." So as a result of this and failure to apply Christian truth to all of life, the secular mind-set monopolizes public debate, Colson maintains.₄ So here we have four highly qualified individuals, living in different times and places, whose thinking is in agreement, voicing concern over the situation in which they found themselves, and it mirrors the concerns we have today.

Admittedly, there is a powerful temptation to exaggerate the importance of one's own times. Colson highlights this, acknowledging that no one can know with certainty whether we face the end of the West as we know it, or not, and that history, as well as the sovereign will of God, is far more complex than we can begin to imagine. So caution is in order, but what we have already observed, and what we are sensing is cultural decay and change beyond what has ever been experienced before in this nation.

"But caution doesn't leave me without convictions," Colson explains. "I believe that we do face a crisis in Western culture, and that it presents the greatest threat to civilization since the barbarians invaded Rome. I believe that today in the West, and particularly in America, the new barbarians are all around us. They are not hairy Goths and Vandals, swilling fermented brew and ravishing maidens; they are not Huns and Visigoths storming or scaling our city walls. No, this time the invaders have come from within. We have bred them in our families and trained them in our classrooms. They inhabit our legislatures, our courts, our film studios, and our churches. Most of them are attractive and pleasant; their ideas are persuasive and subtle. Yet these men and women threaten our most cherished institutions and our very character as a people."[5]

We do right to ask how these new barbarians have managed to invade a nation that spends millions yearly to defend itself from enemy attacks, and yet, without any guns being fired, *we are* being destroyed. Is it too late? What can be done to take back our country?

The seeds of our own barbarian invasion were sown in different soil than that which resulted in Rome's destruction, and so precise parallels between the fall of Rome and the decline of our own civilization, cannot be drawn. While there is much apathy and indifference which surely helped to get this president elected, some of the citizenry of this great country are not standing idly by saying nothing. While we respect the *office* of the President of the United States, when we see and hear the things that are happening, wisdom and right thinking requires that we speak out. I have chosen to let some of those voices speak for themselves here.

THE EMAILS VOICING CONCERNS

If the Internet and email traffic is a fairly accurate assessment of what some of the American population are now thinking about the man they elected to the highest office in the land, then President Obama's approval rating should continue spiraling downward.

One 2009 email sets forth a summary entitled "Observations on the President's Early Days" and shows 23 things reflecting badly on his image. Here are some of those things:

- Offended the Queen of England
- Bowed to the King of Saudi Arabia

- Praised the Marxist Daniel Ortega
- Kissed Hugo Chavez on the cheek
- Endorsed the Socialist Evo Morales of Bolivia
- Announced we would meet with Iranians with no pre-conditions
- Gave away billions to AIG also without pre-conditions
- Doubled our national debt
- Announced a termination of the space defense system the day after the North Koreans launched an ICBM
- Despite the urgings of his own CIA director and the prior four CIA directors, released information on intelligence gathering
- Accepted without public comment the fact that five of his cabinet members cheated on their taxes and two others withdrew after they couldn't take the heat
- Appointed a Homeland Security Chief who quickly identified as "dangers to the nation," groups including veterans of the military, and opponents to abortion on demand...and who ordered that the word "terrorism" no longer be used but instead referred to such acts as "man-made disasters"
- Circled the globe so he could openly apologize for America's greatness
- Told the Mexican President that the violence in their country was because of us
- Politicized the census by moving it into the White House from its Department of Commerce origins
- Authorized the flying of Air Force One over New York City and created 9-11 panic
- Began the process of nationalizing the auto industry and the insurance industry Announced that for intents and purposes the health insurance industry will be nationalized.[6]

There are a few others, but this is a summary of the most disturbing.

An Open Letter Entitled 'YOU SCARE ME' from One of Corporate America's Recognized Leaders in Change Management

Lou Pritchett, well-known public speaker who retired after a successful thirty-six year career as the VP World Sales for Proctor and Gamble, wrote an open letter to President Obama in which each statement begins with "you scare me." [This was widely circulated on the Internet.] Here are some of those statements:

- You scare me, after months of exposure, I know nothing about you; I do not know how you paid for your expensive Ivy League education and your upscale life and housing with no visible signs of support

- You scare me, you did not spend the formative years of youth growing up in America and culturally you are not an American

- You scare me, you lack humility and 'class', blaming others

- You scare me, for over half your life you have aligned yourself with radical extremists who hate America and you refuse to publicly denounce these radicals who wish to see America fail

- You scare me, you are a cheerleader for the 'hate America' crowd and deliver this message abroad

- You scare me, you want to replace our healthcare system with a government controlled one

- You scare me, you want to kill the American capitalist goose that lays the golden egg which provides the highest standard of living in the world; your own political party shrinks from challenging you on your wild and irresponsible spending proposals

- You scare me, you will not openly listen to or consider opposing points of view from intelligent people

- You scare me, you falsely believe that you are omnipotent and omniscient

- You scare me, the media gives you a free pass on everything you do

- You scare me, you demonize and want to silence the Limbaughs, Hannitys, O'Reillys and Becks who offer opposing, conservative points of view

- You scare me, you prefer controlling over governing

- Finally, you scare me because if you serve a second term, I will probably not feel safe in writing a similar letter in four years. 7

A SCHOOL TEACHER'S OPEN LETTER TO THE PRESIDENT

Here are excerpts from a school teacher's open letter to the president:

I have had it with you and your administration, sir. Your conduct on your recent trip overseas has convinced me that you are not an adequate representative of the United States of America collectively or of me personally.

You are so obsessed with appeasing the Europeans and the Muslim world that you have abdicated the responsibilities of the President of the United States of America. You are responsible to the citizens of the United States. You are not responsible to the peoples of any other country on earth.

I personally resent that you go around the world apologizing for the United States telling Europeans that we are arrogant and do not care about their status in the world. Sir, what do you think the First World War and the Second World War were all about if not the consideration of the peoples of Europe? Are you brain dead, what do you think the Marshall Plan was all about? Do you not understand or know the history of the 20th Century?

Where do you get off telling a Muslim country that the United States does not consider itself a Christian country? Have you not read the Declaration of Independence or the Constitution of the United States? This country was founded on Judeo-Christian ethics and the principles governing this country, at least until you came along, come directly from this heritage. Do you not understand this?

Your bowing to the king of Saudi Arabia is an affront to all Americans. Our President does not bow down to anyone, let alone the king of Saudi Arabia. You didn't show Great Britain, our best and one of our oldest allies, the respect they deserve yet you bow down to the king of Saudi Arabia. How dare you, sir! How dare you!

You can't find the time to visit the graves of our greatest generation because you don't want to offend the Germans, but [you do] make time to visit a mosque in Turkey. You offended our dead and every veteran when you gave the Germans more respect than the people who saved the German people themselves. What's the matter with you? I am convinced that you and the members of your administration have the historical and intellectual depth of a mud puddle and should be ashamed of yourselves, all of you.

You are so self-righteously offended by the big bankers and the American automobile manufacturers yet do nothing about the thieves in this situation — Mr. Dodd, Mr. Frank, Franklin Raines, Jamie Gorelic, the Fannie Mae bonuses, and the Freddie Mac bonuses. What do you intend to do about them? Anything? I seriously doubt it.

What about the U.S. House members passing out... millions in bonuses to their staff members, on top of the... millions in automatic pay raises lawmakers gave themselves? I understand the average House aide got a 17 percent bonus. You haven't said anything about that. Who authorized that? I surely didn't! I took a 5 percent cut in my pay to save jobs with my employer.

Executives at Fannie Mae and Freddie Mac will be receiving ... millions in bonuses... In fact, Fannie and Freddie executives have already been awarded... millions — not a bad take. Who authorized that and why haven't you expressed your outrage at this group who are largely responsible for the economic mess we have right now.

I resent that you take me and my fellow citizens as brain-dead and not caring about what you idiots do. We are watching what you are doing and we are getting increasingly fed up with all of you. I also want you to know that I personally find just about everything you do and say to be offensive to everyone of my sensibilities. I promise that I will work tirelessly to see that you do not get a chance to spend two terms destroying my beautiful country.

She signs this: Every real American 8 [her name withheld; however this email was widely circulated around the country]

PATRICK J. BUCHANAN TO OBAMA: A FEW FACTS ABOUT RACE

This is not a subject White Americans bring up in civil conversation, but since the president has said we need to have a conversation about race in America, Pat Buchanan said, "Fair enough. But this time it has to be a two-way conversation. White America needs to be heard from, not just lectured to. This time, the Silent Majority needs to have its convictions, grievances and demands heard. And among them are these:

"First, America has been the best country on earth for black folks. It was here that 600,000 black people, brought from Africa in slave ships, grew into a community of 40 million, were introduced to Christian salvation, and reached the greatest levels of freedom and prosperity blacks have ever known. Wright ought to go down on his knees and thank God he is an American. [Wright was Obama's pastor in Chicago where the doctrine of Christian Black Liberation Theology was preached — a substitute for the Judeo-Christian belief system that uses the Sunday pulpit to preach victimization and promote wealth redistribution.]

"Second, no people anywhere has done more to lift up blacks than white Americans. Untold trillions have been spent since the '60s on welfare, food stamps, rent supplements, Section 8 housing, Pell grants, student loans, legal services, Medicaid, Earned Income Tax Credits and poverty programs designed to bring the African-American community into the mainstream. Governments, businesses and colleges have engaged in discrimination against white folks — with alternative action, contract set-asides and quotas — to advance black applicants over white applicants. Churches, foundations, civic groups, schools and individuals all over America have donated their time and money to support soup kitchens, adult education, day care, retirement and nursing homes for blacks.

"We hear the grievances. Where is the gratitude?

"Barack talks about new 'ladders of opportunity' for blacks. Let him go to Altoona? And Johnstown, and ask the white kids in Catholic schools how many were visited lately by Ivy League recruiters handing out scholarships for 'deserving' white kids? Is white America really responsible for the fact that the crime and incarceration rates for African-Americans are seven times those of white America? Is it really white America's fault that illegitimacy in the African-American community has hit 70 percent and the black dropout rate from high schools in some cities has reached 50 percent?

Is that the fault of white America or, first and foremost, a failure of the black community itself?

"As for racism, its ugliest manifestation is in interracial crime, and especially interracial crimes of violence. Is Barack Obama aware that while white criminals choose black victims 3 percent of the time, black criminals choose white victims 45 percent of the time?

"Is Barack aware that black-on-white rapes are 100 times more common than the reverse, that black-on-white robberies were 139 times as common in the first three years of this decade as the reverse?

"We have all heard ad nauseam from the Rev. Al [Sharpton] about Tawana Brawley, the Duke rape case and Jena. And [it] all turned out to be hoaxes. But about the epidemic of black assaults on white that are real, we hear nothing.

"Sorry, Barack, some of us have heard it all before, about 40 years and 40 trillion tax dollars ago.

"We are a CHRISTIAN NATION even if Mr. Obama says we are not."[9]

[This, too, was widely circulated on the Internet for the entire world to see. Some may consider Buchanan to be racist, but these are facts that can be substantiated, and are worthy of being read.]

"WHEN COLOR TRUMPS CHRISTIANITY"

Yet another widely circulated Internet article by well-known syndicated columnist Star Parker, entitled "When color trumps Christianity," has been praised for its honesty by this well-informed black writer. She informs readers that the president hosted a reception at the White House to celebrate LGBT (Lesbian, Gay, Bisexual, Transgender) Pride month, and that Black Christians should take note and learn a few things about our black president. She said, "As they say, we are what we do. It tells us something that Mr. Obama had no time to host an event for the National Day of Prayer, but he did find time for the other.

"Nor did he accept the invitation to convey greetings and a few remarks to the March for Life event a couple hundred thousand people come to Washington to observe every January."

Ms.Parker called attention to Obama's reasoning equating the homosexual practice movement to the black civil rights movement (which as I pointed out in Chapter 8 is a fallacy), and cited another black Christian woman, Crystal Dixon, who wrote a column in her local paper challenging this position. "Dixon was fired for being uppity enough to write '...I take great umbrage at the notion that those choosing the homosexual lifestyle are civil rights victims...' I cannot wake up tomorrow and not be a black woman.'"

Parker points out other major discrepancies and flawed "logic" in President Obama's comments. "Black Christians have a lot of soul searching to do. We know the pain of black history. But we also must retain clarity that these many injustices were the result of race and color trumping Christian principles?"[10]

"CHANGE"

The well-polished rhetoric of this president shows him to be not only a slick orator, but his brand of change — so vigorously pursued verbally in pre-election campaigning — is nothing but a hostile attack on the Judeo-Christian values and freedoms most Americans hold very dear. This is not "change you can believe in" — but it is change skillfully designed to uproot American culture and replace it with secular, socialist policies. This is tax and spend, move-fast-get-it-done "change" with sweeping ramifications designed to ram big government down the throats of the unsuspecting who voted him in. And the sad part is that they can't take their vote back, not now, in four years, perhaps, unless those holding out their hands for the dole outnumber those who know how to think sensibly. Which says, watch what happens with immigration...and stay alert watching what happens with the census.

Concealment, deceit, calculated maneuverings, flip-flops, relationships with radical leftists — the company he has kept in the past and now still keeps — more regulations by big government, not fewer, more red tape, not less, more bureaucracy, not less, and the list could go on and on of things that need the American people's concern and careful monitoring. *This president's actions are far outside the mainstream values of most Americans* — from his views on abortion and homosexuality to his stated desire to redistribute wealth and everything in between.

OBAMAMERICA!

He promised hope and change — but this Harvard-educated elitist with his grayscale morality clearly shows how bereft he is of wisdom as he continues to throw a wrench into the gears of what was once a remarkable economic machine as he bankrupts America.

On the Obamamerica road to nowhere, the president and his green environmental lobbyists and his kowtowing Democratic Congress, with their ambitious, arrogant, unscrupulous ideologies, will march in lockstep with energy speculators, all the while unable to connect with real families and real people struggling to make ends meet.

Presidents select our Supreme Court justices. As one writer explains: "It will only be a matter of time before Obama is able to tip the balance of the Supreme Court…All but two of the nine Supreme Court judges are over seventy, and one justice is in his late eighties. Within his first term, Obama will likely have the opportunity to appoint anyone he wants to the Court, and the Congress will undoubtedly be willing to do his bidding."11

What does that mean for our country? "Obama will select justices, not for their regard for our laws, but rather, for their political beliefs. And their beliefs about America won't be anything like those of our Founding Fathers. Traditional American values will become a thing of the past, and worse, they will be enshrined in legal 'precedence' — which our president and dutiful minions in Congress will consider untouchable."12 In fact, we saw this very thing embodied by Sonya Sotomeyer in the televised hearings for her confirmation, all we heard was the word "precedence." It was a fallback for her on question after question that was asked. Goodbye checks and balances. Hello Obamamerica! Justice will be changing; Obama wants justices who will act on their emotions, feelings, and "empathy." Americans would do well to heed the statement of Senator Jeff Sessions of Alabama during the Sotomeyer hearings, "Empathy towards one party is always prejudice against another."

AMERICA'S DESCENT INTO MARXISM, SOCIALISM, OR WHATEVER…

The changing scene being hoisted upon the good citizens of this great nation is mind-boggling. What does one call it? The descent has been and is being accomplished as more than one writer describes it, with breathtaking speed. How has it happened? We've been called passive, hapless sheeple (not people) who have been dumbed down through a politicized and substandard education system based on pop culture, rather than the classics. It's been said that we know more about our favorite TV programs than the drama in DC that directly affects our lives. Someone has said that we care more about our "right" to choke down a McDonalds burger or down a Coors than our constitutional rights. This writer expressed the belief that the American populace has surrendered their freedoms and souls to the whims of their elites and betters.

Insulting comments? For those of us — and there are a great number of us — who don't feel we are sheeple — statements like this are very hurtful; we feel wounded by what's taken place and is taking place. Yet there is no denying the truth. And there is more; the Internet spews forth the rage of citizens who say we now have a gangster government, that our country is under siege, and millions don't even realize it.

Michelle Malkin, always incisive, sharp, quick to cut to the chase, pulled no punches when she said "hope and change came to the White House wrapped in brass knuckles," labeling all that's taken place as "White House Thuggery." She suggested one could ask the Congressional Budget Office (CBO) for confirmation, but then Obama's budget director played the heavy and warned the public that the CBO was "exaggerating costs and underestimating savings." The underlying message was "Leave the number fudging to the boss."13

Moderate Blue Dog Democrats revolting against Obamacare's high costs and expansive governmental powers over medical decisions saw the administration's hounds unleashed on them as they sought to be true representatives of the people. Another example of "bullying" according to Malkin, is what happened to former Americorps inspector general Gerald Walpin who "was slimed as mentally incompetent ('confused' and 'disoriented') after blowing the whistle on several cases of community service tax fraud" that included the case of an Obama crony.14

Thankfully there are people like Michelle Malkin, Rush Limbaugh, Cal Thomas, Charles Krauthammer and others already mentioned in this book, who are speaking out, raising their voices as they seek to warn and inform the American people. In speaking of the role of the mainstream media, Rush asserted, "The press has met their Waterloo and it's Obama. They have sacrificed whatever integrity, character, professionalism, ethics that they've had" so now "their total reason — most of them — for existence" is "propping this guy up." He sees "Journalists sitting around with the tingles up their legs all day as they marvel at how Obama is so smooth and elegant."15

The sad story of a president who declared that he and a group of unelected chosen stooges would redesign the entire automotive industry is one that we have had foisted upon us in such a way that we are still reeling. They have enabled financial oligarchs and their henchmen to gorge themselves on trillions of American dollars, in one bailout after another. The rights, duties and powers of the American Congress have been usurped. Both the congress and the people they are supposed to represent have had to take all this and more with barely a whimper as the democratically controlled Congress of America continues to block bi-partisan efforts reflecting the voice of the people.

RACISM IN OBAMAMERICA

Anne Wortham, a highly respected educator, a distinguished professor, known and recognized in higher education, and an author who writes with great clarity in her book *The Other Side of Racism: A Philosophical Study of Black Race Consciousness,* in an email wrote movingly about what she sees happening.

> *Fellow Americans,*
>
> *Please know, I am Black; I grew up in the segregated South. I did not vote for Barak Obama; I wrote in Ron Paul's name as my choice for president. Most importantly, I am not race conscious. I do not require a Black president to know that I am a person of worth, and that life is worth living. I do not require a Black president to love the ideal of America.*
>
> *I cannot join you in your celebration. I feel no elation. There is no smile on my face. I am not jumping with joy. There are no tears of triumph in my eyes. For such emotions and behavior to come from me, I would have to deny all that I know about the requirements of human flourishing and survival — all that I know about the history of the United States of America, all that I know about race relations, and all that I know about Barak Obama as a*

politician. I would have to deny the nature of the "change" that Obama asserts has come to America....

Her brilliant analysis of what brought Obama into the highest office in the land, and her keen insights, make her letter worthy of the widest possible circulation. She decries the fact that Blacks "have chosen to sprint down the road to serfdom that we have been on for over a century...I would have to think it somehow rational that 94 percent of the 12 million Blacks in this country voted for a man because he looks like them (that Blacks are permitted to play the race card), and that they were joined by self-declared "progressive" whites who voted for him because he doesn't look like them."

Her letter goes on:

I would have to wipe my mind clean of all that I know about the kind of people who have advised and taught Barack Obama and will fill posts in his administration — political intellectuals like my former colleagues at the Harvard University's Kennedy School of Government.

I would have to believe that "fairness" is equivalent to justice. I would have to believe that man who asks me to "go forward in a new spirit of service, in a new service of sacrifice" is speaking in my interest. I would have to accept the premise of a man that economic prosperity comes from the "bottom up," and who arrogantly believes that he can will it into existence by the use of government force. I would have to admire a man who thinks the standard of living of the masses can be improved by destroying the most productive and the generators of wealth.

Finally Americans, I would have to erase from my consciousness the scene of 125,000 screaming, crying, cheering people in Grant Park, Chicago irrationally chanting "Yes We Can!" I would have to wipe all memory of all the times I have heard politicians, pundits, journalists, editorialists, bloggers and intellectuals declare that capitalism is dead....

So, you have made history, Americans. You and your children have elected a Black man to the office of the president of the United States, the wounded giant of the world.... The self-righteous welfare statists in the suburbs can feel warm moments of satisfaction for having elected a Black person.

So, toast yourselves: 60s countercultural radicals, 80s yuppies and 90s bourgeois bohemians. Toast yourselves, Black America. Shout your glee Harvard, Princeton, Yale, Duke, Stanford, and Berkeley. You have elected not an individual who is qualified to be president, but a Black man who, like the pragmatist Franklin Roosevelt, promises to do something. You now have someone who has picked up the baton of Lyndon Johnson's Great Society. But you have also foolishly traded your freedom and mine — what little there is left — for the chance to feel good. There is nothing in me that can share your happy obliviousness.16

"GATES OF WRATH"

Then there was the incident in Cambridge where a good neighbor observed two men trying to force open the front door of a neighbor's home, and called 911. By now the story is old news, but it will probably remain in the history books as a case of racial profiling, which it was not. The man seeking to gain entry into the home was an African-American college professor, Henry "Skip" Gates Jr., who was arrested because he acted in a disorderly way to the police officer who just happened to be white. The neighbor who made the phone call did not mention the race of the two men. Sgt. James Crowley was accompanied by two officers — one African-American, one Hispanic. The arresting officer did exactly what was necessary in this situation, but it was blown all out of proportion when President Obama said on nationwide television that he acted "stupidly."

The incident was resolved, the Cambridge Police Department and officers throughout the area, came to Sgt. Crowley's defense, and the president invited the men and some of their friends to the White House for a beer. But what really has been accomplished? Many African-Americans will continue to think they are entitled to mouth off and resist police, and to blame "white society" for their problems, and to peg shortcomings on racism, rather than to take personal responsibility. The stereotypes about white people, and especially about white cops, will continue, and we have a president who showed his bias. So much for the "Beer Summit."

As for Harvard Professor Gates, he once held a political fundraiser for President Obama. Gates is linked to radical black, communist activists. He is a strong supporter of affirmative action and a key member of the reparations movement for the descendants of African slaves. He is well connected to the Democrat Socialists of America.[17]

CHICAGO-STYLE CORRUPTION AND THE WHITE HOUSE

With ethically compromised politicians on Capitol Hill, and the Beltway swarming with Democratic corruption scandals — too numerous to even begin to mention here — as Michelle Malkin says "it's a textbook case of nepotism, self-dealing, back scratching, corporate lobbying, government favors and entrenched incumbency."[18]

And then there's Bill O'Reilly weighing in with his always insightful analysis of what is the then-top-most-talked-about issue of the day, "As President Obama struggles to sell his massive reorganization of the health care industry, it is important to understand what is driving him. This is a classic liberal vs. conservative battle, pitting government money for the poor against rugged individual competition in which the winners get more security than the losers.

"Obama, of course, is a liberal guy — a community organizer…who believes that it is government's responsibility to give [poor] people as much money as possible. Free health care is free money. That puts Obama squarely against Benjamin Franklin who said, 'When the people find they can vote themselves money, that will herald the end of the republic.' Franklin realized that politicians who attempted to buy votes by promising rich entitlements could not look out for the good of the entire country. Thus, an inevitable decline would occur…Benjamin Franklin would not have supported national health care." And neither do the majority of the American people.19

"THE QUEEN AND HER COURT!!" CHANGE COMES TO THE WHITE HOUSE

Information coming across the Internet from the Canada Free Press is startling to say the least. Why the press in this country has not uncovered what our neighbors to the North are finding raises many questions, or could it be that the mainstream media here is so beguiled by this president, his "Queen", and their retinues, that truth and commonsense hide from their consciences.

While Sarah Palin was attacked on every side by the liberal press for every penny she was accused of spending (charges proved to be false), Michelle Obama "gets away with murder," to use an old term expression. "The First Lady requires more than 20 attendants…No, Mrs. Obama does not get paid to serve as the First Lady, and she doesn't perform any official duties. But this hasn't deterred her from hiring an unprecedented number of staffers to cater to her every whim and to satisfy her every request, in the midst of the 'Great Recession.'

"Just think, Mary Lincoln was taken to task for purchasing china for the White House during the Civil War! And Mamie Eisenhower had to shell out the salary herself, for her personal secretary. How things have changed!

"If you're one of the tends of millions of Americans facing certain destitution, earning less than subsistence wages, stocking the shelves at Wal-Mart, or serving up McDonald's cheeseburgers…, prepare to scream and then come to realize that the benefit package for the servants of Miz Michelle are the same as members of the national security and defense departments, and the bill for these assorted lackeys is paid by John Q. Public: (Total this up…it's almost obscene!)"*

This article then gives the names and salaries of 22 (and probably counting) people whose salaries range from $172,000 to the mid-$40,000 range.

The article asks, "Huh? What goes on here? There has never been anyone in the White House at any time that has created such an army of staffers whose sole duties are the facilitation of the First Lady's social life. One wonders why she needs so much help, at taxpayer expense, when even Hillary only had three; Jackie Kennedy, one; Laura Bush, one; and prior to Mamie Eisenhower, social help came from the President's own pocket.

"Note: The above costs do not include makeup artist..., and 'First Hair-stylist,'..., both of whom traveled aboard Air Force One to Europe."[20]

The combined cost of 16 of those people equals $1,191,765. Eight of the salaries were not given. That's your money, dear reader, you, the taxpayer.

A NEW DARK CHAPTER, A NEW NERVOUS AGE

This could be considered a depressing chapter, however, I would like you to think, instead, that it is a clarion call setting forth information that needs to be read and understood in light of the times in which we now find ourselves. That means this is a call to action. Burying our heads in the proverbial sand will not bring about the kind of change which the people of this great nation desire. A dramatic shift has taken place in the country and a word being used to describe what has and is taking place is the word *statism*. It is actually what French historian Alexis de Tocqueville described as *soft tyranny*.[21]

Statism means that the concentration of economic controls and planning is in the hands of a highly centralized government. Advocates of statism are called statists. The Founders of our country understood this — where the few dictate to the many — and they recognized that this is the greatest threat to liberty. Mark R. Levin describes all this brilliantly in his book *Liberty and Tyranny*. This book is a must-read for conservative people who are concerned about the right balance necessary for government control and individual liberty.[22]

Statists have an insatiable appetite for control. Here is a partial list of how they function:

- Redistribute wealth
- Finance welfare programs

- Set prices and production limits
- Create huge public works programs
- Establish pension and unemployment programs
- Expand political alliances
- Create electoral constituencies (unions, farmers, senior citizens,
- Takeover of industries
- Takeover of health care
- Build a culture of conformity and dependency
- Manipulate public perception and seek ways to control the media

You can add to this list from your own observations and experience. This could all come under the title of "the quicksand of *soft tyranny, statism.*"

What is the antidote to what can be seen as living in a state of diminishing liberty? Is statism on the ascendancy and the societal balance tipping away from ordered liberty?

CHAPTER ELEVEN
The Law of Sowing and Reaping

We reap what we sow; we reap after we
sow; we reap more than we sow.

Anonymous

The God who created the world and all therein set certain consistent "laws of nature," that never fail. In fact, if and when these laws are altered, we have a special word for that. The word is miracle! A miracle is when God steps in and alters His natural laws. One law is my focus in this chapter. It is the law of sowing and reaping. This law is consistent throughout the entire world in which we live. Rarely is this law ever broken or altered. When we throw a ball up, it comes down. When we throw watermelon seeds on the ground, watermelons eventually pop up. I am certain you get the message.

With this law in mind let's ask ourselves the question: Is America as a nation and are Americans as a people reaping what we have sown? By now I think you know the answer to this question. Can we acquiesce to a sex-driven-materialistic society driven by self- gratification and greed and expect a tolerable outcome? I think not!

We have sown seeds of socialism culturally and now we seem to be shocked that we are seeing the death of democracy. We have sown seeds of greed and appear to be shocked that society in general cares more about their own immediate gratification than the general well-being of our neighbors. The truth is, we will become outraged that some on Wall Street made fortunes by their dishonesty when, in reality, many Americans would do the same given the opportunity.

The sad fact is we *are* reaping what we have sown. What we have failed to grasp is that God said, "They have sown the wind, and they shall reap the whirlwind" (Hosea 8:7). This speaks both of judgment on the Jewish people, to whom this was addressed, and of the enemy who was to come in and take the land. The picture, however, of sowing when the circumstances are undesirable, is easy to grasp; yes, like a forceful whirlwind sweeping in, what has been sown will be to little or no avail. And the message applies to us. The apostle Paul wrote, "Do not be deceived: God cannot be mocked. A man reaps what he sows" (Galatians 6:7 NIV).

GETTING WHAT WE DESERVE: REAPING THE HARVEST

Here's what I am saying. We *are* now getting what we deserve! Why? you ask. Truth has been compromised by those who despise the God who created us and brought this country into existence. It would be a surprise if you planted corn and pumpkins came up. It's a law of nature to reap what we sow. Every action has results. When our legislators compromise and do not do that which reflects the will of the people whom they are elected to represent, they are sowing to the wind.

It is the people, however, living in a culture which has been so despoiled by what the decision-makers and those in authority have done and are doing that feel and suffer the effects of that which has been sown. We then reap the harvest throughout our society — by irreverent schools where attempts are constantly being made to remove any reference to God from everything, by corporate greed in corporations and those we trusted to invest wisely for us for our futures, by counterproductive legislation and government policies, and by a pervasive and ultra-powerful media. These are just some of the ways the "whirlwind" has caused heartache and wrecked havoc in lives. The activists and those who hate the Judeo-Christian system of values assault us in blatant, and some not so obvious ways.

Our children and grandchildren, for instance, are exposed to rhetoric and in danger of being taken captive by ideas they may not be prepared to handle in school and college. But these children can also be influenced by the television programs that come into our homes, by the hand-held gadgets they seem to be constantly maneuvering with their agile fingers as they play the "games," by the magazines they see on the newsstands, the books they read, and the information that finds its way into our computers and on the Internet.

A grandmother told about coming upon her grandchildren who were playing a video game, one with digitized characters. She peered over their shoulders and was horrified to see the females in bikinis, with the nipples on their boobs plainly visible as their bosoms spilled over, and the guys fondling themselves. This grandmother intervened appropriately.

A friend tells about waiting in the checkout line at the market. Ahead of her was a mother busily talking on her cell phone, paying no attention to her child. The little girl was staring at the magazines. My friend watched as the child's hand went up to the annual bathing suit edition of *Sports Illustrated*. It showed a group of near naked women, their arms only partially crossed over their anatomy. The child put her finger up to the magazine, running it across the lineup of women, and then noticed that the lady with the white hair was watching her. Quickly she put her hand down and turned her head. The mother was too busy chatting on the cell phone to notice what her daughter was doing. My friend turned her head away while she waited in line, but then, turning slightly, observed the child doing it again thinking that now she wasn't being observed. Such is the culture in which we live.

ORAL HISTORIANS TO THE CULTURE

Each generation in a culture searches for its own values. But without the last generation as a backup, especially when the present generation — the parents — may not be passing on the values by which they were raised, children are bereft of the stabilizing influence of godliness, biblical values and right living. Grandparents who live in proximity to their grandchildren can convey what their family stands for by letting grandchildren into their lives passing on family history. Older generations, however, can also be an influence beyond their families. They are the oral historians of the culture and can extend themselves to others in ways that provide a perspective so desperately needed in today's society. I hope you are doing that. If the tide is to be turned in this nation, one of the ways we can help bring that about is by being knowledgeable about what's going on, taking a stand and helping our children, grandchildren, and others who cross our path, gain an understanding of what is taking place. Don't be afraid to speak up when it is appropriate. Do so with graciousness and kindness. Caring about others is not meddling; providing sound words of wisdom born from experience is not intruding. Live with your conscience. Say and do the right things. We can sow seeds that may result in some rootedness in the lives of others. We are not responsible for results, but we are to be faithful.

FOUR SOILS AND THE MEANING OF A PARABLE

Jesus made reference in one of his parables to the law of sowing and reaping. *"A farmer went out to sow his seed. As he was scattering the seed, some fell along the path, and the birds came and ate it up. Some fell on rocky places, where it did not have much soil. It sprang up quickly, because the soil was shallow. But when the sun came up, the plants were scorched, and they withered because they had no root. Other seed fell among thorns, which grew up and choked the plants, so that they did not bear grain. Still others fell on good soil. It came up, grew and produced a crop, multiplying thirty, sixty, or even a hundred times....*

"When he was alone, the Twelve and the others around him asked him about the parables...Then Jesus said to them, 'Don't you understand this parable?...The farmer sows the word. Some people are like seed along the path, where the word is sown. As soon as they hear it, Satan comes and takes away the word that was sown in them. Others, like seed grown on rocky places, hear the word and at once receive it with joy. But since they have no root, they last only a short time. When trouble or persecution comes because of the word, they quickly fall away. Still others, like seed sown among thorns, hear the word, but the worries of this life, the deceitfulness of wealth and the desires for other things come in and choke the word, making it unfruitful. Others, like seed sown on good soil, hear the word, accept it, and produce a crop — thirty, sixty or even a hundred times what was sown" (Mark 4:3-8, 10, 13-20 NIV).

In the culture of that time, seed was sown by hand, so the farmer would sow liberally, and enough would fall on good ground to ensure the harvest. The four soils represent four different ways people respond to the truths of God's Word. We must strive to be like good soil in every area of our lives at all times. First-century disciples were not too unlike us today in respect to what takes place in the busyness of our lives. The truths of the Word and how it can help us in our work, our relationships, and the way we react to the culture, can get crowded out if we are not careful. We listen with our ears, but there is a deeper kind of listening with the mind and heart that is necessary to gain spiritual understanding to influence the world around us. I think we can also glean from this parable that not all seed is going to fall on good soil, but this must not discourage us as we faithfully sow. Leave the results with God; you be faithful. God's Word is the seed that falls.

As Christians, living in a culture of disbelief, unbelief, and outright scorn and hatred for what we stand for as revealed to us in the Bible, we will face hostility and rejection, but we can stand firm and remain fixed as we show Christian graces and Christlike character. Our strength comes from God Himself as we stand for righteousness. We can have hope because God is still in control. His plan will be fulfilled. God's people flourish during times of oppression and conflict as we call upon the Lord. It is time to pray, refuse to compromise, step up and speak out for Jesus Christ and personal holiness!

THE WORLD NEEDS YOU

You may think you are only one person living in this culture, in what has been called "the sea of mendacity," meaning deception and falsehood, so what can one person do! Things are just not what they should be. God's standards for righteousness have been and are being assaulted from every side. Righteousness encompasses everything that makes up the opposite of wickedness. It is no wonder then that we are sensitive to what takes place. But one with God is a majority.

The world needs us as mature Christians. All through history, God's people have carried His Word into one dangerous arena after another. They did this not because they felt themselves to be well trained or especially equipped, but because they felt it was the right thing to do. In the next chapter I will set forth principles and make some suggestions as to what you, an average layperson, can do. "Not that we are sufficient of ourselves to think any thing as of ourselves; but our sufficiency *is* of God" (2 Corinthians 3:5).

CHAPTER TWELVE
Hope for Today and the Future

If I find in myself a desire which no experience in this world can satisfy, the most probable explanation is that I was made for another world.

C. S. Lewis
in *Mere Christianity*[1]

If you have stayed with me this far in this book, then you know the guided tour of the realities we have faced and are facing as a nation are very challenging. But all is not lost in this journey for those of us who realize there is more to life than the here and now. We, who call ourselves Christians, know there is an ongoing battle taking place "in the heavenlies" that plays itself out on earth. It is warfare that has been raging since the beginning of time. We may get battle weary at times, but we have not been left defenseless, and there is an unseen host warring on our behalf. When strength wanes, the likelihood is that we have not called on God for His help or, in truth, we may be neglecting His Word, the Bible, which instructs us, and are not in communication with Him through prayer.

America at the Tipping Point is more than the title of this book; it is a part of the reality confronting Americans. But America is, as she always was, a Christian nation. Her heritage remains, and her birthright can be reclaimed if we, as individual Christ-ones, do what must be done. God's prophetic clock is indeed ticking; we are nearer today than we have ever been before to end-time events signaling Christ's return.

So as we come to the end of the journey through this book, I must raise the question: Has America gone too far down the road to our own destruction? As Americans we have made choices each time we've arrived at a tipping point, and it appears that some very poor, immoral and detrimental choices have been made. But, have we gone too far? Can the situation in this country be turned around? Is there hope for this once great nation?

The truth is we each have to answer that question. Maybe we have passed the point of no return as a nation, but what about me, what about you? Are we to throw up our hands in disgust and adopt a defeatist mentality? God forbid! While we may not be able to reverse the course America and the world is on, we have a responsibility and a call to stand firm until the end of our time on earth. Therefore, what can I, what can you, what can we do?

"MADE FOR ANOTHER WORLD"

C. S. Lewis, in his much-valued book, *Mere Christianity,* in writing on the subject of hope, said: "I must keep alive in myself the desire for my true country, which I shall not find till after death; I must never let it get snowed under or turned aside; I must make it the main object of life to press on to that other country and to help others to do the same."[2]

That, too, should be our aim throughout our days here on Planet Earth; included in that desire must be a loving concern for others. To that end, as we follow the Bible's directives, we will want to be both the salt and light in an ever-decaying and darkening world. We have been given a mandate to fight the good fight for our families, our country, and supremely for God who has entrusted this responsibility to us. To that end, we should not be hiding in our churches, as some are doing, holding forth the view that Christians "shouldn't be involved in politics, that this is worldly, that we shouldn't declare war on our culture." This begs questions: If Christians don't defend righteousness, then who **is** going to do that? When we encounter violations of God's moral laws, and we know the truth, and no one is stepping up to tackle injustice and evil, how can we possibly **not** respond?

Are we just to accept political labels, judicial intimidation, and threats of more and more government intrusion into our lives and churches without speaking and stepping out for what we know is right, fair and against that which is wrong? While our hope ultimately lies in God setting things right and in Christ's return, we need not accept defeat now while idly awaiting His soon coming. We are to be about the Lord's work with the fervor and courage these troubled times demand. How can we do that? And what really is hope — hope for today and the future?

CAN HOPE BE DEFINED?

Can hope adequately be defined? Yes, it can. Here's what the dictionary says: 1. To cherish a desire with expectation of fulfillment. 2. *archaic* **TRUST. 1:** To long for with expectation of obtainment.

You get the idea. *Strong's Exhaustive Concordance of the Bible* declares that hope is the expectation of future good. It provides 105 biblical references to the word hope. God's Word gives us reason to be hopeful about hope. We can be a public voice for the eternal truths of God.

ACTION IDEAS FOR ENGAGEMENT IN THE CULTURE

Here are some action ideas for engagement in the culture that are definitely not all-inclusive or definitive for everyone; they are basic and really quite simple to implement.

- Pay attention to what is taking place — locally, nationally, personally (how what is happening may impact you and your family). Be informed. Read, study and listen.

- Inform others. Find those who agree that what you see and hear happening is in violation of moral values and ethical standards; this should include friends and neighbors. Then discuss ways whereby a grassroots effort could help to bring about change, and do what is possible to implement the agreed-upon views. Change may not be forthcoming immediately, but at least let your voices be made known and live with your conscience.

Doable Ideas Contributing Your Time and Skill for a Righteous Cause

- Encourage people to be registered to vote.
- Support candidates running for office that you know are reputable.

- Run for office.

- Write letters to advertisers when you see something being advertised that is unacceptable.

- Contact the media — print, radio, TV. Alert them to what has come to your attention; or voice your concern about issues. If there is a local or national organization that is taking a stand and working to bring about change, contact them; join also with them as they seek ways to make a difference; inform them if you are encountering situations that require a concerted national effort.

- Be a Christian watchdog. At this perilous time in our nation's history, pay attention to what an intrusive and aggressive government is saying and doing. When legislation is pending, write and voice your concerns as it affects traditional values and religious liberty.

- When you bump up against things that are a violation of God's Word, speak up, write letters, emails, and make calls.

- Sign petitions that reflect your concerns.

- Volunteer to serve in your local schools; run for the school board after you become somewhat known for your volunteering efforts.

- Pray without ceasing; alert others to the need for prayer about whatever it is that has come to your attention or God has imprinted upon your heart that needs prayer.

- Seek ways with others of like mind to hold your representatives in Washington accountable.

- Read bills that you can download from your computer.

- Discern who the "enemies" are of what America has always stood for.

- Question with boldness, and when you speak, do so without fear in a respectful way.

- Hold onto truth and offer hope.

Tom Minnery in his book, *Why You Can't Stay Silent: A Biblical Mandate to Shape Our Culture,* asks these perturbing questions: "Should today's Christian people engage or not? Should the church stand as a bulwark athwart the quickening river of unrighteousness, or should it simply pull survivors, one by one, to a heavenly higher ground and ignore the gathering flood? What happens in the church when some say yes and some say no, when believers who want to yank evil out by its roots dislodge a landslide of controversy? What does history tell us?"3

Minnery presents many accounts, both biblical and from the pages of history, setting forth what individuals and organizations have done as they confronted immense social conditions. He provides examples and the stories of such people as England's William Wilberforce, and John Newton (does the song *Amazing Grace* come to mind?), Congressman Henry Hyde (in more recent history), John Wesley the evangelist, Jerry Falwell (the Moral Majority), Theodore Weld (the crusade against slavery), Harriet Beecher Stowe (the author of *Uncle Tom's Cabin*; President Lincoln, upon meeting her said, "So this is the lady who made this big war?"); William and Catherine Booth (the Salvation Army founders); and the many who have been waging the battle against abortion, pornography, homosexuality, and other social ills.

HOLDING ONTO TRUTH AND OFFERING HOPE

Our responsibility as those who know the truth that sets people free (John 8:32), is to share this wonderful news so they, too, "can lay hold of the hope set before us" which the Bible says is an "anchor of the soul" (Hebrews 6:18, 19). We have this "living hope because of the abundant mercy of Jesus Christ and His resurrection from the dead" (1 Peter 1:3).

The Psalms speak of this hope we have in so many places as, for instance, in these beautiful words: "Be of good courage, And He shall strengthen your heart, All you who hope in the Lord" (Psalm 31:24).

The whole world longs for a steadfast hope, and God will enable and use us as dispensers of that hope. I encourage you to study God's Words of hope, and trust Him to help you be a messenger of that hope to those you encounter. Stand firm and do not grow weary in well doing. In the end, we WIN!

"Your Word I have hidden in my heart,
That I might not sin against You…
Strengthen me according to Your word.
I have chosen the way of truth;…
Teach me, O Lord, the way of your statutes,
And I shall keep it to the end…
Let Your mercies come also to me,
O Lord—
Your salvation according to Your word.
So shall I have an answer for him who reproaches me,
For I trust in Your word.
And take not the word of truth utterly out of my mouth,
For I have hoped in Your ordinances…
And I will walk at liberty
For I seek Your precepts.
I will speak of Your testimonies…
And will not be ashamed…
You are my hiding place and my shield;
I hope in Your word…
Uphold me according to Your word,
that I may live;
And do not let me be ashamed of my hope"

(Psalm 119:11, 28b, 30a, 33, 41-43, 45, 46, 114, 116, 117a NKJ).

APPENDICES

APPENDIX 1

D ue to the fact our public schools have become the foremost battle ground in the war on culture I wanted to include this very informative and helpful material prepared by Dr. Chuck Missler, founder of Koinonea House and used with permission. Chuck outlines what Christians can do and why they can do it. I urge the reader not to be intimidated by hearsay but rather know the facts and share these truths with others.

RELIGIOUS FREEDOM AND PUBLIC SCHOOLS —

"Congress shall make no law respecting an establishment of religion, or prohibiting the free exercise thereof; or abridging the freedom of speech..." — First Amendment to the U.S. Constitution

Public schools across America are warming up again, and the smells of pencil shavings, new backpacks and cafeteria lunches will soon fill the halls. With the sorrow of leaving summer behind and the excitement of new things ahead there comes a perennial question of how the US Supreme Court will allow God to fit into it all. After the landmark 1962 Supreme Court decision *Engle vs Vitale*, which ended school-sponsored prayer in American public schools, there has been confusion over whether students or teachers are allowed to pray, read their Bibles or engage in other religious activity on school grounds.

In August of 1995, the Secretary of Education issued guidelines on Religious Expression in Public Schools to clarify which activities were and were not constitutional and to prevent religious discrimination against public school students.

On February 7, 2003, then-Education Secretary Rod Paige issued a similar set of guidelines, updated under the No Child Left Behind Act of 2001 to make adherence to the guidelines a requirement for receiving federal funding. Under the guidelines, schools must annually submit in writing to their state education agency that they are following the guidelines in good faith. Those who fail to attest to their compliance in writing, and those who have been faulted for failing to obey the guidelines, risk losing their federal funding. The guidelines clarify the religious rights of public school students during school hours. They note:

"As the Court has explained in several cases [ie *Santa Fe Indep. Sch. Dist. v. Doe* (2000) and *Board of Educ. v. Mergens* (1990)], 'there is a crucial difference between government speech endorsing religion, which the Establishment Clause forbids, and private speech endorsing religion, which the Free Speech and Free Exercise Clauses protect.'"

Schools must neither encourage nor discourage religious expression, and they may not discriminate against activity simply because it is religious in nature. As long as students initiate the religious activity themselves, and as long as the religious expression falls within the schools' rules of order, it cannot be discriminated against.

According to the Supreme Court in *Everson v. Board of Education* (1947), the First Amendment "requires the state to be a neutral in its relations with groups of religious believers and non-believers; it does not require the state to be their adversary. State power is no more to be used so as to handicap religions than it is to favor them."

So, how does that fit into everyday life at school?

Free Time:

If students have free time during which they may engage in non-religious activities — recess, lunch-time, and so forth — then they may also use that time for religious activities such as prayer or Bible reading.

Class Assignments:

Students may express their religious beliefs in class assignments — written, oral, or art work — without discrimination because the work is religiously oriented. Teachers are to grade assignments based on their academic quality without penalty or reward for religious themes or content.

Clubs:

Students may form prayer groups or religious clubs "to the same extent that students are permitted to organize other non-curricular student activities groups." According to the Supreme Court in *Good News Club v. Milford Central School* (2001), that includes access to school facilities. If a school's policy only permits clubs directly related to the curriculum, like history or math groups but not jazz or sailing groups, then it could also prohibit a religious club that is not connected to school curriculum.

Advertising:

If schools allow non-religious school groups to promote their activities through posters or school newspapers, then religious groups, like Bible or prayer clubs, must also be allowed to promote their activities.

Teachers:

According to the Supreme Court in *Engel v. Vitale* (1962) and *School Dist. of Abington Twp. v. Schempp,*(1963), public school teachers represent the state and may not lead classes in prayer or Bible reading. Teachers also may not compel children to engage in religious activities. Yet, teachers do retain their First Amendment rights in the public schools. While teachers must remain neutral and neither encourage or discourage their students' religious expression, teachers may pray or study the Bible by themselves or with other teachers.

Student Speeches:

There has been a lot of controversy over how to handle student speeches that contain religious themes. The guidelines offer a position that might surprise a few people. They say:

"Student speakers at student assemblies and extracurricular activities such as sporting events may not be selected on a basis that either favors or disfavors religious speech. Where student speakers are selected on the basis of genuinely neutral, evenhanded criteria and retain primary control over the content of their expression, that expression is not attributable to the school and therefore may not be restricted because of its religious (or anti-religious) content."

In *Lee v. Weisman* (1992), the Supreme Court prohibited schools from specifically choosing somebody to pray at assemblies, and schools cannot pick students to speak because of religious or anti-religious motivation. However, as the Supreme Court explained in *Board of Educ. v. Mergens* (1990), "The proposition that schools do not endorse everything they fail to censor is not complicated." That applies even to public settings with public audiences. If it dares, a school can offer a neutral disclaimer saying that the content of student speeches is solely their own and not the school's, freeing students to speak about religious or non-religious or anti-religious themes as they choose.

Kevin Hasson, president of the Washington-based Becket Fund for Religious Liberty, commented, "What the guideline says is that if is truly student-initiated — if it's not rigged by the school district somehow — then the First Amendment protects it."

And if a school chooses strict pre-approval of all graduation speeches? Families and students may pray and talk about God freely at baccalaureate services.

Schools and teachers, parents and students should discuss these guidelines and become familiar with the religious freedoms students have in the public schools. Americans need to know they do not "shed their constitutional rights to freedom of speech or expression at the schoolhouse gate."

APPENDIX 2

TIME LINE OF WORLDWIDE SCHOOL SHOOTINGS

The following table lists the worldwide school shootings from 1996 to the present. Find the date, location, and a short description of each incident. This is taken from www.infoplease.com

Feb. 2, 1996 — Moses Lake, Wash.
Two students and one teacher killed, one other wounded when 14-year-old Barry Loukaitis opened fire on his algebra class.

March 13, 1996 — Dunblane, Scotland
16 children and one teacher killed at Dunblane Primary School by Thomas Hamilton, who then killed himself. 10 others wounded in attack.

Feb. 19, 1997 — Bethel, Alaska
Principal and one student killed, two others wounded by Evan Ramsey, 16.

March 1997 — Sanaa, Yemen
Eight people (six students and two others) at two schools killed by Moham-mad Ahman al-Naziri.

Oct. 1, 1997 — Pearl, Miss.
Two students killed and seven wounded by Luke Woodham, 16, who was also accused of killing his mother. He and his friends were said to be outcasts who worshiped Satan.

Dec. 1, 1997 — West Paducah, Ky.
Three students killed, five wounded by Michael Carneal, 14, as they partici-pated in a prayer circle at Heath High School.

Dec. 15, 1997 — Stamps, Ark.
Two students wounded. Colt Todd, 14, was hiding in the woods when he shot the students as they stood in the parking lot.

March 24, 1998 — Jonesboro, Ark.

Four students and one teacher killed, ten others wounded outside as Westside Middle School emptied during a false fire alarm. Mitchell Johnson, 13, and Andrew Golden, 11, shot at their classmates and teachers from the woods.

April 24, 1998 — Edinboro, Pa.

One teacher, John Gillette, killed, two students wounded at a dance at James W. Parker Middle School. Andrew Wurst, 14, was charged.

May 19, 1998 — Fayetteville, Tenn.

One student killed in the parking lot at Lincoln County High School three days before he was to graduate. The victim was dating the ex-girlfriend of his killer, 18-year-old honor student Jacob Davis.

May 21, 1998 — Springfield, Ore.

Two students killed, 22 others wounded in the cafeteria at Thurston High School by 15-year-old Kip Kinkel. Kinkel had been arrested and released a day earlier for bringing a gun to school. His parents were later found dead at home.

June 15, 1998 — Richmond, Va.

One teacher and one guidance counselor wounded by a 14-year-old boy in the school hallway.

April 20, 1999 — Littleton, Colo.

14 students (including killers) and one teacher killed, 23 others wounded at Columbine High School in the nation's deadliest school shooting. Eric Harris, 18, and Dylan Klebold, 17, had plotted for a year to kill at least 500 and blow up their school. At the end of their hour-long rampage, they turned their guns on themselves.

April 28, 1999 — Taber, Alberta, Canada

One student killed, one wounded at W. R. Myers High School in first fatal high school shooting in Canada in 20 years. The suspect, a 14-year-old boy, had dropped out of school after he was severely ostracized by his classmates.

May 20, 1999 — Conyers, Ga.

Six students injured at Heritage High School by Thomas Solomon, 15, who was reportedly depressed after breaking up with his girlfriend.

Nov. 19, 1999 — Deming, N.M.
Victor Cordova Jr., 12, shot and killed Araceli Tena, 13, in the lobby of Deming Middle School.

Dec. 6, 1999 — Fort Gibson, Okla.
Four students wounded as Seth Trickey, 13, opened fire with a 9mm semi-automatic handgun at Fort Gibson Middle School.

Dec. 7, 1999 — Veghel, Netherlands
One teacher and three students wounded by a 17-year-old student.

Feb. 29, 2000 — Mount Morris Township, Mich.
Six-year-old Kayla Rolland shot dead at Buell Elementary School near Flint, Mich. The assailant was identified as a six-year-old boy with a .32-caliber handgun.

March 2000 — Branneburg, Germany
One teacher killed by a 15-year-old student, who then shot himself. The shooter has been in a coma ever since.

March 10, 2000 — Savannah, Ga.
Two students killed by Darrell Ingram, 19, while leaving a dance sponsored by Beach High School.

May 26, 2000 — Lake Worth, Fla.
One teacher, Barry Grunow, shot and killed at Lake Worth Middle School by Nate Brazill, 13, with .25-caliber semiautomatic pistol on the last day of classes.

Sept. 26, 2000 — New Orleans, La.
Two students wounded with the same gun during a fight at Woodson Middle School.

Jan. 17, 2001 — Baltimore, Md.
One student shot and killed in front of Lake Clifton Eastern High School.

Jan. 18, 2001 — Jan, Sweden
One student killed by two boys, ages 17 and 19.

March 5, 2001 — Santee, Calif.
Two killed and 13 wounded by Charles Andrew Williams, 15, firing from a bathroom at Santana High School.

March 7, 2001 — Williamsport, Pa.
Elizabeth Catherine Bush, 14, wounded student Kimberly Marchese in the cafeteria of Bishop Neumann High School; she was depressed and frequently teased.

March 22, 2001 — Granite Hills, Calif.
One teacher and three students wounded by Jason Hoffman, 18, at Granite Hills High School. A policeman shot and wounded Hoffman.

March 30, 2001 — Gary, Ind.
One student killed by Donald R. Burt, Jr., a 17-year-old student who had been expelled from Lew Wallace High School.

Nov. 12, 2001 — Caro, Mich.
Chris Buschbacher, 17, took two hostages at the Caro Learning Center before killing himself.

Jan. 15, 2002 — New York, N.Y.
A teenager wounded two students at Martin Luther King Jr. High School.

Feb. 19, 2002 — Freising, Germany
Two killed in Eching by a man at the factory from which he had been fired; he then traveled to Freising and killed the headmaster of the technical school from which he had been expelled. He also wounded another teacher before killing himself.

April 26, 2002 — Erfurt, Germany
13 teachers, two students, and one policeman killed, ten wounded by Robert Steinhaeuser, 19, at the Johann Gutenberg secondary school. Steinhaeuser then killed himself.

April 29, 2002 — Vlasenica, Bosnia-Herzegovina
One teacher killed, one wounded by Dragoslav Petkovic, 17, who then killed himself.

October 28, 2002 — Tucson, Ariz.
Robert S. Flores Jr., 41, a student at the nursing school at the University of Arizona, shot and killed three female professors and then himself.

April 14, 2003 — New Orleans, La.
One 15-year-old killed, and three students wounded at John McDonogh High School by gunfire from four teenagers (none were students at the school). The motive was gang-related.

April 24, 2003 — Red Lion, Pa.
James Sheets, 14, killed principal Eugene Segro of Red Lion Area Junior High School before killing himself.

Sept. 24, 2003 — Cold Spring, Minn.
Two students are killed at Rocori High School by John Jason McLaughlin, 15.

Sept. 28, 2004 — Carmen de Patagones, Argentina
Three students killed and 6 wounded by a 15-year-old Argentininan student in a town 620 miles south of Buenos Aires.

March 21, 2005 — Red Lake, Minn.
Jeff Weise, 16, killed grandfather and companion, then arrived at school where he killed a teacher, a security guard, 5 students, and finally himself, leaving a total of 10 dead.

Nov. 8, 2005 — Jacksboro, Tenn.
One 15-year-old shot and killed an assistant principal at Campbell County High School and seriously wounded two other administrators.

Aug. 24, 2006 — Essex, Vt.
Christopher Williams, 27, looking for his ex-girlfriend at Essex Elementary School, shot two teachers, killing one and wounding another. Before going to the school, he had killed the ex-girlfriend's mother.

Sept. 13, 2006 — Montreal, Canada
Kimveer Gill, 25, opened fire with a semiautomatic weapon at Dawson College. Anastasia De Sousa, 18, died and more than a dozen students and faculty were wounded before Gill killed himself.

Sept. 27, 2006 — Bailey, Colo.
Adult male held six students hostage at Platte Canyon High School and then shot and killed Emily Keyes, 16, and himself.

Sept. 29, 2006 — Cazenovia, Wis.
A 15-year-old student shot and killed Weston School principal John Klang.

Oct. 3, 2006 — Nickel Mines, Pa.
32-year-old Carl Charles Roberts IV entered the one-room West Nickel Mines Amish School and shot 10 schoolgirls, ranging in age from 6 to 13 years old, and then himself. Five of the girls and Roberts died.

Jan. 3, 2007 — Tacoma, Wash.
Douglas Chanthabouly, 18, shot fellow student Samnang Kok, 17, in the hallway of Henry Foss High School.

April 16, 2007 — Blacksburg, Va.
A 23-year-old Virginia Tech student, Cho Seung-Hui, killed two in a dorm, then killed 30 more 2 hours later in a classroom building. His suicide brought the death toll to 33, making the shooting rampage the most deadly in U.S. history. Fifteen others were wounded.

Sept. 21, 2007 — Dover, Del.
A Delaware State Univesity Freshman, Loyer D. Brandon, shot and wounded two other Freshman students on the University campus. Brandon is being charged with attempted murder, assault, reckless engagement, as well as a gun charge.

Oct. 10, 2007 — Cleveland, Ohio
A 14-year-old student at a Cleveland high school, Asa H. Coon, shot and injured two students and two teachers before he shot and killed himself. The victims' injuries were not life-threatening.

Nov. 7, 2007 — Tuusula, Finland
An 18-year-old student in southern Finland shot and killed five boys, two girls, and the female principal at Jokela High School. At least 10 others were injured. The gunman shot himself and died from his wounds in the hospital.

Feb. 8, 2008 — Baton Rouge, Louisiana
A nursing student shot and killed two women and then herself in a classroom at Louisiana Technical College in Baton Rouge.

Feb. 11, 2008 — Memphis, Tennessee
A 17-year-old student at Mitchell High School shot and wounded a classmate in gym class.

Feb. 12, 2008 — Oxnard, California
A 14-year-old boy shot a student at E.O. Green Junior High School causing the 15-year-old victim to be brain dead.

Feb. 14, 2008 — DeKalb, Illinois
Gunman killed five students and then himself, and wounded 17 more when he opened fire on a classroom at Northern Illinois University. The gunman, Stephen P. Kazmierczak, was identified as a former graduate student at the university in 2007.

Sept. 23, 2008 — Kauhajoki, Finland
A 20-year-old male student shot and killed at least nine students and himself at a vocational college in Kauhajok, 330km (205 miles) north of the capital, Helsinki.

Nov. 12, 2008 — Fort Lauderdale, Florida
A 15-year-old female student was shot and killed by a classmate at at Dillard High School in Fort Lauderdale.

March 11, 2009 — Winnenden, Germany
Fifteen people were shot and killed at Albertville Technical High School in southwestern Germany by a 17-year-old boy who attended the same school.

APPENDIX 3

ABORTION PROCEDURES

There are three different procedures that are used to abort a baby during the first trimester of pregnancy, or the first three months of the nine month gestation period. A lot happens during the first trimester of pregnancy that is neatly summed up by the abortionists in the word "embryo" until week seven and then "fetus", once the baby reaches week eight. While technically accurate, these words alone mask the obvious humanness of the living child developing in the mother's womb. They would rather the public not know the details of what is happening in the womb during even the first three WEEKS of pregnancy, much less the first trimester.

THE JOURNEY TO DEATH — THE FIRST TRIMESTER

For our purpose, let's examine what happens to the baby during her journey toward death. During just the first three weeks of pregnancy the nervous system, kidneys, liver, intestines, and other organs are beginning to form, the backbone and spinal column are beginning to take form, and the baby has attached itself to the wall of the mother's uterus. All of this development has occurred even before the mother has missed her menstrual cycle and begins to suspect that she is pregnant.

By the end of the fourth week, the baby has its own heartbeat that can be seen on an ultrasound of the mother's abdomen, and the brain is taking form. By week seven, baby's facial features are formed and a mouth, nose, and tongue are prominent. The muscular system is also present, a retina has formed over the eyes, and the baby is pumping its own blood, and even moving in the mother's womb. By week eight, the baby has arms, legs, and brainwaves that can be measured, and hair begins to appear on her head. When she is nine weeks old, she can turn somersaults and even jump inside mother's womb! She can squint to close out light, swallow and move her tongue, and she can even frown when she is unhappy. Week ten sees a completely developed heart, which is more than I can say for most abortionists, and little teeth are forming in the gums. By week twelve, the end of just the first trimester of pregnancy, the baby has completely formed vocal chords, and she will sometimes cry silently. The baby's brain is fully formed, and she may be seen on ultrasound sucking her thumb. Tragically for the baby who is aborted during the twelfth week of pregnancy, it can also feel sensations at this point. How many women having an abortion during the first trimester do you think are told that their baby can likely feel the hellish ordeal it is about to endure? Not many, I would wager. [1]

All of this development takes place just in the first trimester of pregnancy, the trimester when most abortions are performed. With this in mind, let's look at some of the abortion procedures most commonly used during this stage of pregnancy.

Suction Aspiration

Suction Aspiration is the most common form of abortion used during the first trimester of pregnancy. During the procedure, the cervix is dilated and the abortionist uses a hollow tube with a knife-edged tip called a suction curette, which is connected via a transparent tube to a powerful vacuum that will create suction twenty-nine times more powerful than a household vacuum cleaner. Inserted into the womb, the suction curette will be used to tear the baby and the placenta into small pieces that are sucked through the tube into a bottle for disposal. The innocent baby who has spent the last many weeks frowning, crying, sucking its thumb, and jumping in her mother's womb is brutally sliced to bits and reduced to medical waste in a matter of minutes. [2]

Dilation and Curettage (D&C)

Dilation and Curettage, or D&C, is similar to the suction method described above, but instead of dismembering the baby using high-power suction, a loop shaped knife is used to slice the baby up into pieces. The placenta is then scraped from the uterine wall and scooped out along with the mutilated baby, and discarded. This method causes more bleeding for the mother than suction aspiration, and runs a higher risk of uterine perforation and infection. The abortion industry would have us believe that abortions are simple procedures with no risk to the mother, but, as with any surgical procedure, there are always risks of complications and infection.3 This is only one of the reasons I find it beyond absurd that minors are allowed to have an abortion without their parent's consent. Were the child to develop a fever following the procedure, her parents would likely assume she had the flu, and would have no idea that her fever could be a sign of infection caused by the surgical procedure she had done without their knowledge. This is why school nurses are, in every other case, required to notify the parents before providing medical treatment to their children. Parents need to know when their children are sick, and whether they've taken any medications. When it comes to abortion, however, "choice" comes before safety.

RU 486

RU 486, commonly known as the French abortion pill, is actually made up of two powerful synthetic hormones, mifepristone and misoprostol. These hormones are used to chemically induce an abortion in women who are five to nine weeks pregnant. This method of abortion requires the mother to make three trips to the abortion clinic. In the first visit she is given a physical exam, and if she has no medical issues that would preclude her from taking RU 486, she is given the RU 486 pills at the end of the visit.

While the mother goes about her life over the next thirty-six to forty-eight hours, the RU 486 blocks the action of progesterone in her body, which is the natural hormone that maintains the rich nutrient lining of her uterus. The end result is that the baby, who is attached to the uterine wall, starves to death. One to two days after her first appointment, the mother goes back for her second appointment and is given a dose of artificial prostaglandins to induce uterine contractions, and cause her to deliver the dead baby. In most cases, the baby will be fully aborted in the abortion clinic during the four- hour waiting period that follows administration of the prostaglandins. However, 30 percent of mothers don't respond that quickly, and the aborted baby will be expelled at home, at work, or wherever she happens to be when the uterine contractions happen. This can happen as much as five days later. Imagine being in a shopping mall, or at work when the remains of your baby are finally delivered from the womb. What a horrifying and potentially embarrassing experience. While I feel sympathy for these mothers, many of whom know little about the life they are exterminating, have made their choice.

In addition to this process of waiting, RU 486 can have several serious side effects, including severe bleeding, nausea, vomiting, pain, and even death. At least one woman in France died after being given the drug and others have suffered heart attacks, and required emergency surgery following the procedure. The book is not written on RU 486, and many more studies are needed to know the full extent of the drugs adverse affects. Some research indicates RU 486 may even cause future miscarriages, or deformities in later children. What other field of medicine, if you can call abortion that, would even consider using a drug with these side effects and possible consequences? I guess one shouldn't expect to find responsible and ethical practices in a profession that specializes in death.

These are the abortion methods most often used during the first trimester of pregnancy, or before the twelfth week. Sadly, in most cases, the mother is never informed about the gory details of the procedures listed above before she makes her choice. She's never been told about the stages of development of a human baby, even in the first trimester, and she's been led to believe that she carries inside her a lifeless piece of tissue called a fetus that doesn't really become a baby until some magical point in time during the birthing process. These procedures are horrific enough, but the realities of abortion only get more tragic as the stage of the woman's pregnancy gets later.

THE SECOND TRIMESTER

When the mother has entered her second trimester of pregnancy, different procedures must be used to perform an abortion, because the baby is changing rapidly and is now in a more advanced stage of development. By the time the mother enters the second trimester of pregnancy, her baby's muscles have become more developed, and she will start to feel the flutters and kicks of her child moving around in the womb. Incredibly, at fifteen weeks the baby has developed her adult taste buds, and may even be able to taste her mother's meals! Imagine that. Your child's first time making a face at the taste of vegetables may have actually happened in the womb. By sixteen weeks her little face has eyebrows and eyelashes, and she can kick and move about the womb. At eighteen weeks she blinks, grasps things with her hands, which will soon have fingernails and unique fingerprints, and moves her mouth.

When the pregnancy reaches twenty weeks, the baby could survive outside the womb if born prematurely. You would think at this point the argument over whether an unborn child is actually a living human being with a right to live would end, but sadly even the ability to survive outside the womb does not protect an unborn child from the deadly tentacles of the abortion industry.

A twenty-week old baby can hear and recognize their mother's voice, and the mother's ultrasound at this point will tell her whether she is going to have a little boy or a little girl. Once again, how can anyone at this point deny the presence of a human life? Can it be a boy or a girl, and yet not human? Even so, abortions are frequently performed during the second trimester, taking the lives of millions of unique and specially created children. Their lives are snuffed out using barbaric techniques, that most assuredly cause the baby unimaginable pain.

Dilation and Evacuation (D&E)

If you thought these procedures couldn't get worse, they can. What remains to be told gets increasingly disturbing, but please bear with me. It is because these facts are not known by the public, that the media, politicians, and the abortion industry are able to propagate the lie that an abortion is a clean, simple procedure that none of us should feel any guilt or shame about. It remains a part of our culture precisely because discussing the horrible truths of what an abortion is makes us uncomfortable. We are, therefore, too often willing to leave these dark secrets hidden within the walls of the abortion clinics that have become nearly as common as the local McDonalds in cities across the country. As disturbing as it is, the facts must be brought out of the shadows.

The D&E is a procedure that's used up to the eighteenth week of pregnancy. Instead of the loop-shaped knife used in the D&C, a pair of forceps is inserted into the womb and used to crush and break the baby's bones, and then tear the baby into pieces. In the process, the spine is usually snapped and the skull must be crushed in order to remove the pieces of the baby through the dilated cervix. The idea is that as the baby grows and becomes stronger, more draconian tools must be used to do the same job. If you think about it, the process isn't really that much different from the brutal torture performed on innocent Iraqi's in Uday Hussein's torture chambers prior to their liberation by U.S. forces. Our nation will send its sons and daughters to liberate the suffering people of Iraq, but turn a blind eye to our own torture chambers. Those who decry the treatment of Al Qaeda prisoners in Guantanamo Bay, Cuba, might spend some time in an abortion clinic and apply the same moral principals.

Salt Poisoning (Saline Injection)

After sixteen weeks, when enough fluid has accumulated in the womb, salt poisoning is sometimes used to kill the baby. A long needle is used to inject a saline solution into the sac that envelops the baby inside the womb. Over the next hour, the baby will swallow this deadly solution and be poisoned to death. However, the baby doesn't just endure poisoning, as the saline also acts as a corrosive and burns off the baby's top layer of flesh. At this age, when the baby would likely survive outside the womb, she can no doubt feel the excruciating pain of having her skin burned away, while the mother usually remains unaware of the horrors she has just inflicted on an innocent child, and waits for her baby to die. After twenty-four hours the mother will go into labor and give birth to either a dead baby, or in many cases, a live baby who has been severely burned. That's right. There are many documented cases of these babies surviving the poisoning. In most cases they are simply left to die, however a few have actually survived the abortion and gone on to be adopted. Gianna Jessen was one of these babies.

On April 22, 1996, Gianna Jessen stood before the Constitution Subcommittee of the House Judiciary Committee and shared a story of great tragedy, hope, and survival. Gianna was nineteen-years-old, living in Tennessee, and had cerebral palsy. She stood before the House subcommittee and announced, "I am adopted. I have cerebral palsy. My biological mother was seventeen- years-old and seven and one-half months pregnant when she made the decision to have a saline abortion. I am the person she aborted. I lived instead of died."

Fortunately for Gianna, the abortion doctor was not there when her mother arrived for her abortion. Her mother delivered her earlier than expected following the saline injection, so when she arrived, she was alive instead of dead. Gianna acknowledged that, if the abortionist had been present when she was born, she was sure she would not be here today, as his job was to take her life, not sustain it.

This brave young woman stood before politicians, many of whom were pro-abortion, and said, "some have said I am a 'botched abortion,' a result of a job not well done." She went on to describe the hysteria, she was informed many years later, that must have existed in the abortion clinic when she was born, and the staff nurse who called emergency medical services and had Gianna transferred to a hospital. Weighing only two pounds when she arrived, Gianna would remain in the hospital for two months. Not much hope was given for her survival. Today, however, babies much smaller than Gianna routinely survive, if given the chance.

You might be thinking that the mother decided to have the abortion because she didn't want a child with cerebral palsy. Not so. Gianna was a healthy, normal baby girl before the abortion. It was the saline poisoning that caused her cerebral palsy. However, Gianna never stopped being a fighter. Through the prayers and dedication of her foster mother and many others, Gianna beat all odds. Eventually she learned to sit up, crawl, then stand. Eventually, she learned to walk, even though doctors had told her foster mother she never would. The Department of Social Services resisted releasing Gianna to be adopted, but finally allowed her foster mother's daughter, Diana De Paul, to adopt her a few months after she began walking.

After four surgeries, Gianna can now walk without assistance, and even joked that, after nineteen-years of falling, she had learned to fall gracefully. This precious child of God told the House subcommittee that "she was happy to be alive." "I almost died," she said. "Every day I thank God for life. I do not consider myself a byproduct of conception, a clump of tissue, or any other of the titles given to a child in the womb. I do not consider any person conceived to be any of those things," she continued. "I have met other survivors of abortion. They are all thankful for life. Only a few moths ago I met another saline abortion survivor. Her name is Sarah. She is two-years-old. Sarah also has cerebral palsy, but her diagnosis is not good. She is blind and has severe seizures. Sarah was also injected in the head with saline during the abortion. When I speak, I speak not only for myself, but for the other survivors, like Sarah, and also for those who cannot yet speak..."

How could anyone vote to continue providing legal abortions on demand after hearing a testimony like that? Yet, politicians have voted to continue this practice. They've voted against legislation that would protect babies that are born alive, as did President Barack Obama when he voted against an Illinois state bill that would have protected babies born alive following a failed abortion. Showing no concern for the newborn baby's life, he said, "Let's trust the guy who just botched the abortion to determine whether or not he actually did botch the abortion." In other words, Obama prefers to let the abortion provider correct his mistake by letting the baby die of exposure and neglect. Of course, we're talking about a man who once said that determining when a baby's life begins is "above his pay grade." Considering his final solution for a living child outside the womb, I would argue that the Presidency is also above his pay grade. I believe these politicians can live with themselves, knowing what they are doing, because human life in our world has been completely devalued. So much so that even babies who are born alive are often left to die in the corner of an abortion clinic, not unlike the Jews left to die in the gas chambers of Auschwitz.

THE THIRD TRIMESTER

In the last weeks of pregnancy, even most abortionists will admit that the mother carries in her womb a child who, if born, would stand a very high probability of survival. At six months the baby looks very much like it would, if allowed to be born three months later. She is practicing breathing in preparation for that first breath that she may never get to take. During these last three months of pregnancy, the abortionist may use either prostaglandin chemical abortion, or a hysterectomy to abort the child.

Prostaglandin Chemical Abortion

Using chemicals developed by UpJohn Pharmaceutical Co., a particularly violent birthing process is induced. Contractions much more severe than natural contractions are induced by the injected drugs, which often, as is the intention, kill the baby as it is born. The violent nature of the contractions has even been known to decapitate the child, as it passes through the birth canal. Sometimes, however, the babies survive the violent trip out of the womb, and are born alive. Here again, most of them are left to die.

Hysterectomy/Cesarean Section

In this procedure, the umbilical cord, which supplies oxygen to the baby, is cut prior to birth, and the baby is allowed to suffocate in the womb. The death normally takes place inside the mother, but, once again, babies are sometimes delivered alive. Those babies are tossed aside and allowed to die of suffocation or exposure.

Final Stages of Development

After thirty weeks, the baby is sleeping most of the time, and even experiencing REM sleep (dreaming). I wonder what this new little life dreams of. I'm positive it isn't dreaming of the horrors abortionists have come up with to end its life at this late stage of pregnancy. Even in the very last weeks of pregnancy, women decide

they don't want their child, and choose to have an abortion, rather than deliver the life they have been carrying inside them for nearly nine months. Up until 2003, these women were able to seek out the most controversial form of abortion, though all of them should be controversial, to terminate their very late-term pregnancy. Most of us have heard the term partial-birth abortion. It is a form of abortion so gruesome that President Bush finally signed an act banning the practice in 2003, and it was actually upheld by the Supreme Court for a change. While the procedure is illegal in most cases, it is still a legal procedure where its use is "necessary" to protect the health of the mother. However, doctors have testified before Congress that, in this day and age, abortion is NEVER necessary to save the life of the mother, and would in fact be an added danger in a troubled pregnancy.

Sadly, this legislation hasn't meant a true ban on partial birth abortion, as lawyers have managed to make "the health of the mother" mean just about anything. If carrying her child to term will cause depression for the mother, this can be deemed psychologically harmful enough to justify a partial birth abortion under the law. The law could have been a step in the right direction in the fight to protect these innocent lives, but our legal system always finds a way. While the public might believe the practice is no longer legal, you can be sure these kinds of abortions are still performed if the mother doesn't want to have her child badly enough. Lawyers can always find a reason her health would be too adversely affected.[4]

Partial Birth Abortion

Guided by ultrasound imagery of the baby, the helpful abortionist uses forceps to grab the baby's legs and then pulls them out into the birth canal. He then delivers the baby's entire body except for the head. Considering what the abortionist is about to do, I can understand them wanting to conceal their evil somewhat by stopping the delivery at this point. It also probably wouldn't fare well for their business to have the mother hear the baby scream or cry — something it's been practicing for several weeks now. The abortionist now jams the forceps into the back of the baby's skull and opens them far enough to leave a gouge in the back of the baby's head. After removing the forceps, a suction catheter is inserted into the wound and the baby's brain is suctioned out, collapsing the skull. The rest of the now-dead baby is then delivered. Just inches away from being fully born, an innocent child is brutally murdered because his or her mother felt an "unwanted pregnancy" was justification for doing so. Only the pro-death movement in this country could believe, and convince millions of other people, that a baby is not a human being, simply because its head still remains in the birth canal, stifling its scream, and temporarily hiding its brutal murder.

That folks, is what abortion really is. It's more than contraception, it's far worse than birth control, and it is never the humane answer to a mother's first choice — the one she had when she got pregnant to begin with. You might wonder how we've come to this place in our national journey, where innocent life can mean so little, and human beings can perform such horrific acts on millions of children. The history that led us to this place is not one the abortion industry wants you to know about. They work very hard to separate themselves from their past, and the past of their founders.

ENDNOTES

1.   "Pregnancy Tips: Fetal Development during the First Trimester," Essortment, Lisa Vella, 2002, http://www.essortment.com/lifestyle/pregnancytipsn_sgdl.htm.

2.   "Abortion Methods, Surgical Abortions," Life Site News, http://www.lifesitenews.com/abortiontypes/

3.   "Abortion — Some Medical Facts," National Right to Life, http://www.nrlc.org/abortion/ASMF/asmf.html.

4.   "U.S. Supreme Court Ruling Upholding Partial-Birth Abortion Ban Act," National Right to Life, 4/18/2007, http://www.nrlc.org/press_release_new/Release041807.html

APPENDIX 4

Culture Links:

The Networks, E-mails and Blogs from the Left Reporting on the Killing of Late-term Abortionist Dr. George Tiller, on May 31, 2009

This is an abbreviated summation of the reporting done by the networks, e-mails, and bloggers from the Left on the killing of George Tiller, the Kansas doctor notorious for his commitment to performing late-term abortions.

One of the headlines declared: **Media: Tiller a Martyr, Abortion Not Killing, and Pro-Lifers are Crazy.** That one headline is pretty much a tell-all, the reporting portraying abortionist Tiller as a courageous defender of women. By his own count, Tiller performed 60,000 abortions. His clinic, Women's Health Care Services in Wichita, was [supposedly] one of three clinics in the United States that offered abortions after the 21st week of pregnancy.

In reporting this story, the news media had much to say about this doctor who helped to provide women with the "right" to end their pregnancies; but these same media sources had little, or nothing, to say about the lives he ended. By failing to explain what Toller's work actually entailed, reporters did nothing to help their audiences understand why this man was targeted. That cannot be considered objective reporting.

The Aura of Martyrdom

Broadcast coverage by the Left media noted past attempts people have made to disrupt Tiller's work, for instance there was the bombing of his clinic in the 1980s, and then a 1993 attack in which he was shot in both arms. Each story increased the aura of martyrdom surrounding his killing on May 31, 2009.

ABCs "World News Sunday" and "Good Morning America" reports featured footage of a 1991 interview in which he stated, "I have a right to go to work. What I am doing is legal. What I am doing is moral. What I am doing is ethical. And you're not going to run me out of town."

"The Huffington Post," one of the most virulent Left-wing blog sites, made Tiller out to be a humanitarian, describing how he was the only doctor who could help a friend of hers who wanted to terminate her pregnancy after learning the baby would be born deformed. That friend, Jill Brooke wrote, "says a prayer for Dr. Tiller almost every day," and called him "a hero" after learning about his murder.

THE "SERVANT OF WOMEN"

NBC "Nightly News" featured Tiller stating, "You simply cannot retreat when you're committed." Eleanor Smeal, currently the president of the Feminist Majority Foundation and former president of the National Organization for Women (NOW), told NBC, "People don't understand the need for this service, that women's lives are saved, but he did. And he was brave enough to keep going."

CBS interviewed Tiller's lawyer, Dan Monnat, during the June 1 "Early Show," where he was asked, "Can you explain why Dr. Tiller continued his practice all these years, despite all the harassment?" Monnat answered, in part, "Both Dr. Tiller and his family continually asked the question, if Dr. Tiller is not here to serve a woman's right to choose, who will be here to do it? There are only a handful of late-term abortion providers that remain in the United States, and in the world. Most of them have been terrorized and run off by the protestors."

ABCs host Diane Sawyer gave Lee Thompson, another Tiller lawyer, the same opportunity to portray him as a misunderstood servant of women, when she asked, "Given the controversy and given the danger, why was he committed to doing this? What was it exactly that he wanted to make sure that he was accomplishing?? Thompson replied, "The fact that he is one of, if not the only one of too very few doctors who perform these services speaks to his dedication and his courage throughout his life."

"DOMESTIC TERRORISM AT ITS WORST"

Bloggers attempted to equate Dr. Tiller's death with terrorism. Michelle

Kraus of *"The Huffington Post,"* described Dr. Tiller as "an unassuming man who did not choose his destiny," and that his death was "an act of domestic terrorism at its worst."

Another blogger tried to link Tiller's death to terrorism: "Not surprisingly, his killer is strongly suspected to be affiliated with the 'pro-life' movement. If that's the case, it makes Tiller the tenth person in the United States to be murdered by anti-choice terrorists."

Cristina Page, writing in *"The Huffington Post"* wrote: "One can only conclude that like terrorist sleeper cells, these extremists have now been set in motion. Indeed the evidence is already there. The chatter, the threats, the hate-filled rhetoric are abundant."

WHEN ABORTION BECOMES "DEADLY"

According to abortion proponents, abortion only becomes "deadly" when it causes the shooting of an abortion doctor. ABCs host Diane Sawyer teased the "Good Morning America" report with "The abortion debate turns deadly." The question could rightly be asked: Diane, when did it turn deadly?

"World News Sunday" anchor David Muir referred to Tiller's killing as "cold-blooded."

NBC reported President Barack Obama's response on the "Today" and "Nightly News" segments where his statement, in part, read, "However profound our differences as Americans over difficult issues, they cannot be resolved by heinous acts of violence."

There you have it — "deadly," "cold-blooded," and a "heinous act of violence."

LINKAGE TO THE DEPARTMENT OF HOMELAND SECURITY'S REPORT

Not surprisingly, at the People for the American Way's "Right Wing Watch," someone gleefully connected Dr. Tiller's murder to the Department of Homeland Security's (DHS) report, "Rightwing Extremism Current Economic and Political Climate Fueling Resurgence in Radicalization and Recruitment." That report, which insulted and angered, rightfully, many Christians and veterans' groups, singled out returning Iraq veterans and mentioned "groups and individuals that are dedicated to a single issue, such as opposition to abortion or immigration." A man by the name of Kyle, who tried to connect these dots, reported "All of the caterwauling eventually lead DHS to pull that report, but in light of the details emerging about Scott Roeder, the man arrested in the killing of physician George Tiller, it seems as if the report — far from being an offensive attack on Christians and anti-abortion activists — was remarkably timely and accurate."

HOW MOST PRO-LIFE ADVOCATES PROTEST

Only the most inflammatory responses were reported by much of the media while "anti-abortion" organization's statements condemning the actions that resulted in Tiller's death, were left out. In actuality, statements from major pro-life organizations revealed a different story, that the pro-life community truly views all loss of human life as a tragedy. The National Life to Right Committee's Executive Director, Dr. David N. O'Steen, affirmed that all life is sacred, in his statement, "The pro-life movement works to protect the right to life and increase respect for human life. The unlawful use of violence is directly contrary to that goal."

Wendy Wright, president of Concerned Women for America, reminded people of how most pro-life advocates protest: "Through the years, hundreds of thousands of pro-lifers have prayed for George Tiller, peacefully tried to persuade him to end his killing of innocent children and exploitation of women, and actively worked to enforce the laws of Kansas. We were guided by the hope that he would change his ways and find forgiveness in Jesus Christ."

APPENDIX 5

THE TEACHINGS OF THE JUDEO-CHRISTIAN TRADITION

According to the Scriptures Regarding Perversions of Sex, Including Homosexuality

Genesis 18   God announces the coming destruction of Sodom and Gomorrah and His judgment upon them because "their sin is very grievous" (vs. 20).

Genesis 19:1-29   Verses 4 and 5 reveals the degradation of the city of Sodom; it is a sickening scene. The chapter deals graphically with the manner in which God, the righteous Judge, deals with the problem of *sin*, and homosexuality is a sin. This is a very important chapter in the Bible for this present generation in which we are living today.

Jesus referenced what happened to these cities in the Gospel accounts: See Matthew 10:15; 11:23, 24; Mark 6:11; and Luke 10:12; 17:29. These cities are also referenced in 2 Peter 2:6; Jude 7; and Revelation 11:8. Throughout the Old Testament, reference is made to Sodom and Gomorrah and the *sin* which brought them down.

Leviticus 18 deals with sexual relations with relatives (vs. 6), a blanket statement forbidding this; and it goes on to amplify on sundry sexual sins that are prohibited in the rest of the chapter. Verse 22, in particular, says, "You shall not lie with a male as with a woman. It is an abomination." The remainder of the chapter deals with the abominable and atrocious sins which the people of the land committed, and the word *abominations* specifically are used four times. It speaks of the *land as being defiled*, so much so that they would be *"vomited"* out of existence. Why? Because God says so, declaring "I *am* the Lord your God" (vs. 30).

Leviticus 20 portrays the "Holiness Code" and verse 13 again emphasizes the *abomination* of homosexuality.

In the New Testament, Romans 1:18-32 shows God's indictment of the world, showing why man needs the righteousness of God. Garry

Kinder, well-known Bible teacher of a class that has been meeting more than thirty years in a Dallas Country Club, speaking on these verses, emphasizes that "When the government condones something, we, as Christians, have to listen to what the Bible condemns."

These verses are generally regarded as the most important biblical texts on homosexuality:

"For the wrath of God is revealed from heaven against all ungodliness and unrighteousness of men, who suppress the truth in unrighteousness, because what may be known of God is manifest in them, for God has shown it to them…because although they knew God, they did not glorify Him as God, nor were they thankful, but became futile in their thoughts, and their foolish hearts were darkened…they exchanged the truth of God for the lie, and worshiped and served the creature rather than the Creator, who is blessed forever. Amen. For this reason God gave them up to vile passions. For even their women exchanged the natural use for what is against nature. Likewise also the men, leaving the natural use of the woman, burned in their lust for one another, men with men committing what is shameful, and receiving in themselves the penalty of their error which was due. And even as they did not like to retain God in their knowledge, God gave them over to a debased mind, to do those things which are not fitting…" (verses 18, 19, 21, 25, 26, 27, 28).

Dr. J. Vernon McGee's commentary on verse 28 is instructive: "Anybody who tells me that he can be a child of God and live in perversion, live in the thick mire of our contemporary permissiveness, is not kidding anyone but himself. If he will come to Christ, he can have deliverance…How much longer will God tolerate it and be patient with us? He has judged great nations in the past who have gone in this direction. Man has a revelation from God, but he flagrantly flaunts it be defying the judgment of God against such sins. He continues to practice them and applauds and approves those who do the same."[iii]

I Corinthians 6:9-11; and I Timothy1:9-10 are warnings against moral laxity.

Homosexual rights advocates, their academic defenders, and Bible revisionists, would have us believe that it is time to amend our thinking of traditional Jewish and Christian attitudes toward homosexuality. As many point out, once you begin to be selective about which moral prescriptions you obey and which you dismiss then you are no longer using the Bible as your standard of behavior. That is totally unacceptable.

Of Himself, Jesus said, "Do not think that I came to destroy the Law or the Prophets, I did not come to destroy but to fulfill. For assuredly, I say to you, till heaven and earth pass away, one jot or one tittle will be no means pass from the law till all befulfilled" (Matt. 5:17, 18). Jesus' point is that every word of the Old Testament is vital and will be fulfilled, and the same is true for the New Testament. I like what Congressman Dannemeyer said: "Cultural relativism was obviously fashionable in Sodom and is fashionable again today." The Bible remains as the ultimate authority for belief and action.

WHERE WE ARE TODAY

A friend relates that while listening to a Fox Newscast and an interview being conducted with an openly "gay" priest being named a Bishop, the TV reporter mentioned the biblical account of Sodom and Gomorrah, and another priest standing alongside his friend, scoffed, "Oh that, the Bible is just an old outdated book."

A few days later, this friend was having dinner with a friend and her granddaughter, and she related the above incident. The granddaughter said, "Well, why can't homosexuals get married to each other? I've been listening to TV too, and I'm hearing a lot about this. If you're going to tell me the Bible says it's not right, then I want to know chapter and verse."

They were able to tell her. But the thinking of young and old, and in between, is being impacted by what's taking place in the culture. When situations like this occur, it is precisely at such times that we must step up to the plate and affirm what we know to be right and true, and if we don't know the chapter and verse, at least we should be able to say, "I'll find out for you and let you know." We have a great biblical and historical heritage, and we must defend both without fear or hesitation.

When Jesus was being questioned by the Pharisees and His disciples, He referred to the Sodom account, and added, "When the Son of Man comes will He really find faith on the earth?" (Luke 18:8).

This doesn't seem to give much promise for improved spiritual conditions in the world before Christ returns.

In this appendix, we have endeavored to provide for you an easily accessible listing of those biblical passages that relate to homosexuality.

> *Listen to me, you who know righteousness,*
> *You people in whose heart is My law:*
> *Do not fear the reproach of men,*
> *Nor be afraid of their insults...*
> *My righteousness will be forever,*
> *And my salvation from generation to generation.*
>
> **(Isaiah 51:7, 8b)**

Appendix 6

EIGHT METHODS FOR THE DESTRUCTION OF AMERICA

A speech by the former Governor of Colorado Dick Lamm

We know Dick Lamm as the former Governor of Colorado. In that context his thoughts are particularly poignant. In August 2009 there was an immigration overpopulation conference in Washington, DC , filled to capacity by many of America 's finest minds and leaders. A brilliant college professor by the name of Victor Hansen Davis talked about his latest book, 'Mexifornia,' explaining how immigration — both legal and illegal was destroying the entire state of California . He said it would march across the country until it destroyed all vestiges of The American Dream.

At that same meeting, moments later, former Colorado Governor Richard D. Lamm stood up and gave a stunning speech on how to destroy America. The audience sat spellbound as he described eight methods for the destruction of the United States. He said, "If you believe that America is too smug, too self-satisfied, too rich, then let's destroy America. It is not that hard to do. No nation in history has survived the ravages of time. Arnold Toynbee observed that all great civilizations rise and fall and that 'An autopsy of history would show that all great nations commit suicide."

"Here is how they do it,"Lamm said: "First, to destroy America , turn America into a bilingual or multi-lingual and bicultural country. History shows that no nation can survive the tension, conflict, and antagonism of two or more competing languages and cultures. It is a blessing for an individual to be bilingual; however, it is a curse for a society to be bilingual. The historical scholar, Seymour Lipset, put it this way: 'The histories of bilingual and bicultural societies that do not assimilate are histories of turmoil, tension, and tragedy: Canada , Belgium , Malaysia , and Lebanon all face crises of national existence in which minorities press for autonomy , if not independence, Pakistan and Cyprus have divided. Nigeria suppressed an ethnic rebellion. France faces difficulties with Basques, Bretons, Corsicans and Muslims.'"

Lamm went on: "Second, to destroy America , invent 'multicultural-ism' and encourage immigrants to maintain their culture. Make it an arti-cle of belief that all cultures are equal; that there are no cultural differences. Make it an article of faith that the Black and Hispanic dropout rates are due solely to prejudice and discrimination by the majority. Every other expla-nation is out of bounds.

"Third, we could make the United States an 'Hispanic Quebec ' with-out much effort. The key is to celebrate diversity rather than unity. As Benjamin Schwarz said in the Atlantic Monthly recently: 'The apparent success of our own multi-ethnic and multicultural experiment might have been achieved not by tolerance but by hegemony. Without the dominance that once dictated ethnocentriy and what it meant to be an American, we are left with only tolerance and pluralism to hold us together.'" Lamm said, "I would encourage all immigrants to keep their own language and culture. I would replace the melting pot metaphor with the salad bowl metaphor. It is important to ensure that we have various cultural subgroups living in America enforcing their differences rather than as Americans, emphasiz-ing their similarities.

"Fourth, I would make our fastest growing demographic group the least educated. I would add a second underclass, unassimilated, undereducated, and antagonistic to our population. I would have this second underclass have a 50 percent dropout rate from high school.

"My fifth point for destroying America would be to get big foundations and business to give these efforts lots of money. I would invest in ethnic identity, and I would establish the cult of 'Victimology.' I would get all minorities to think that their lack of success was the fault of the majority. I would start a grievance industry blaming all minority failure on the majority plation.

"My sixth plan for America's downfall would include dual citizenship, and promote divided loyalties. I would celebrate diversity over unity. I would stress differences rather than similarities. Diverse people worldwide are mostly engaged in hating each other — that is, when they are not killing each other. A diverse, peaceful, or stable society is against most historical precet. People undervalue the unity it takes to keep a nation together. Look at the ancient Greeks. The Greeks believed that they belonged to the same race; they possessed a common language and literature; and they worshipped the same gods. All Greece took part in the Olympic games.. A common enemy, Persia, threatened their liberty. Yet all these bonds were not strong enough to overcome two factors: local patriotism and geographical conditions that nurtured political divisions. Greece fell. 'E. Pluribus Unum' — from many, one. In that historical reality, if we put the emphasis on the 'pluribus' instead of the 'Unum,' we will 'Balkanize' America as surely as Kosovo.

"Next to last, I would place all subjects off limits. Make it taboo to talk about anything against the cult of 'diversity.' I would find a word similar to 'heretic' in the 16th century — that stopped discussion and paralyzed thinking. Words like 'racist' or 'xenophobe' halt discussion and debate. Having made America a bilingual/bicultural country, having established multi-cultum, having the large foundations fund the doctrine of 'Victimology,' I would next make it impossible to enforce our immigration laws. I would develop a mantra: That because immigration has been good for America , it must always be good. I would make every individual immigrant symmetric and ignore the cumulative impact of millions of them."

In the last minute of his speech, Governor Lamm wiped his brow. Profound silence followed. Finally he said, "Lastly, I would censor Victor Hanson Davis's book *Mexifornia.* His book is dangerous. It exposes the plan to destroy America. If you feel America deserves to be destroyed, don't read that book."

There was no applause. A chilling fear quietly rose like an ominous cloud above every attendee at the conference. Every American in that room knew that everything Lamm enumerated was proceeding methodically, quietly, darkly, yet pervasively across the United States today. Discussion is being suppressed. Over 100 languages are ripping the foundation of our educational system and national cohesiveness. Even barbaric cultures that practice female genital mutilation are growing as we celebrate 'diversity.' American jobs are vanishing into the Third World as corporations create a

Third World in America — take note of California and other states, to date, ten million illegal aliens and growing fast. It is reminiscent of George Orwell's book *1984*. In that story, three slogans are engraved in the Ministry of Truth building: 'War is peace,' 'Freedom is slavery,' and 'Ignorance is strength.'

Governor Lamm walked back to his seat. It dawned on everyone at the conference that our nation and the future of this great democracy is deeply in trouble and worsening fast. If we don't get this immigration monster stopped within three years, it will rage like a California wildfire and destroy everything in its path, especially The American Dream.

NOTES

CHAPTER 1

1. "Notes taken from the Video *America's Godly Heritage*," by David Barton, Comments by Dale Costner, http://www.biblebb.com/files/HERITAGE.HTM.

2. *Barack Obama Stops Wearing American Flag Lapel Pin*, Fox News, October 04, 2007, http://www.foxnews.com/story/0,2933,299439,00.html

3. *The New England Primer*, Wikipedia, 7/5/2008, http://en.wikipedia.org/wiki/The_New_England_Primer

4. "Notes Taken from the Video *America's Godly Heritage,*" by David Barton, Comments by Dale Costner, http://www.biblebb.com/files/HERITAGE.HTM

5. *Roosevelt's Religion*, Christian Fichthorne Reisner, 1922 (New York: Abingdon Press).

6. *Realizable Ideas*, Theodore Roosevelt, 1911

CHAPTER 2

1. "The Supreme Court and Religion in American Life — From 'Higher Law' to 'Sectarian Scruples'," Tames Hitchcock, Princeton University Press, 2004, pg. 72.

2. "Glimpses #187: The Truth about the Wall of Separation," Christian History Institute, 2005, http://chi.gospelcom.net/GLIMPSEF/Glimpses2/glimpses187.shtml.

3. "Original Intent, the Courts, the Constitution, and Religion," David "Barton, Wallbuilders Press, 2000, pg. 13.

4. "Jefferson to the Danbury Baptists, 1802," The RJ&L Religious Liberty Archive, 08/08/2005, http://www.churchstatelaw.com/historicalmaterials/8_8_5.asp.

5. Ibid.

6. "Faith and Politics, and de Tocqueville's American Prophecy," Ben Rast, Contender Ministries, http://www.contenderministries.org/articles/world events/faithpolitics.php

7.   Ibid

8.   "Judicial Review — United States," Wikipedia, 07/24/2008, http://en.wikipedia.org/wiki/Judicial_review#United_States

9.   "Everson v. Board of Education," Wikipedia, 05/16/2008, http://en.wikipedia.org/wiki/Everson_v._Board_of_Education.

10.   *America's God and Country,* William J. Federer (St. Louis, MO: Amerisearch, Inc., 2000) 651-652.

CHAPTER 3

1.   Engel v. Vitale — Further Readings, Law Library — American Law and Legal Information, http://law.jrank.org/pages/6483/Engel-v-Vitale.html

2.   Burge, pg. 45

3.   "Maricopa School District says no to religious content on fliers," Alliance Defense Fund, 7/24/2008, http://www.alliancedefensefund.org/main/general/print.aspx?cid=4622.

4.   "Demonic Artwork Okay, Scripture and Cross — No Way!" Alliance Defense Fund,   04/15/2008,   http://www.alliancedefensefund.org/main/general/print.aspx?cid=4471.

CHAPTER 4

1.   *Situation Ethics: The New Morality,* J. Fletcher (Philadelphia, PA: Westminster, 1966), pg. 26.

2.   John Shelby Spong, Wikipedia, 8/16/2008,

3.   *The Influence of Eastern Mysticism,* Dave Hunt (Eugene, OR: Occult Invasion, Harvest House, 1998), Ankerburg Theological Research Institute, http://www.johnankerbert.org/Articles/_PDFArchives/new-age/NA2W0802.pdf, pg. 2.

4.   Ibid.

5.   "FBI charges Florida professor with terrorist activities," CNN U.S., February 20th, 2003, http://www.cnn.com/2003/US/South/02/20/professor.arrest/index.html

6. "Den of Thieves," David Horowitz, March 24, 2006, http://www.discoverthe networks.org/individualProfile.asp?indid=2229

7. "Unearthing the Weather Underground," Joseph Morison Skelly, National Review Online, October 17, 2008, http://article.nationalreview.com/?q=NTRm OTk2ZWZjNjEwZDVlMmFlYjc3Y2EwYmJmNTdiMzg=&w=MA==

8. Ibid.

9. "A Victims View of Obama's Friend Bill Ayers," Moonbattery, August 29, 2008, http://www.moonbattery.com/archives/2008/08/a_victims_view.html

10. "Elections," American Education Research Association, 2008, http://www. aera.net/AboutAERA/Default.aspx?menu_id=18&id=321.

11. "Moral Relativism — Neutral Thinking?" http://moralrelativism.com

12. Biography of Roosevelt by Edmund Morris.

13. "Bill Clinton Presidential Campaign, 1992," Wikipedia, 8/15/2008, http://en. wikipedia.org/w/index.php?title=Bill_Clinton_presidential_campaign,_1992

14. "Paula Jones," Wikipedia, 8/15/2008, http://en.wikipedia.org/wiki/Paula_Jones

15. "Divorce Rate by Country," Nation Master, 2008, http://www.nation master.com/graph/peo_div_rat-people-divorce-rate

16. "The Unexpected Legacy of Divorce: A 25-Year Landmark Study — The Love they Lost: Living With the Legacy of Our Parent's Divorce," William Vogal, Ph.D. American Psychiatry Association, 08/2001, http://psychservices.psychiatry online.org/cgi/content/full/52/8/1108.

17. "Divorce Doesn't Go Away — The new Wallerstein-Lewis study traces 25 years of the effects of divorce on children," Claudia Miller, http://www.4children. org/news/198divo.htm

18. "Moral Dilemmas of Early Adolescents of Divorced and Intact Families," Burnett Tysse, Journal of Early Adolescence, 1933.

19. Testimony of Michael Tanner; Director Health and Welfare Studies, Cato Institute. Before the Finance Committee, United States Senate, March 9, 1995, http://www.cato.org/testimony/ct-ta3-9.html.

20. "The Hidden Effects of Divorce on Children," http://www.dealwithdivorce.com/effects-divorce/hidden-effects-divorce/01

21. "Out-of-Wedlock Birth Rate Reaches All-Time High," Mike Stobbe, Associated Press, 11/22/2006, http://www.dailytexanonline.com/home/index.cfm?event=displayArt.

22. Ibid.

23. Press Release for PBS Special: "Let's Get Married" aired 11/14/2008, http://www.pbs.org/wgbh/pages/frontline/press/2106.html.

24. "Statistics of the United States", U.S. National Center for Health Statistics, 1990, 2005.

25. "Encouraging Marriage and Discouraging Divorce," Patrick F. Fagan, Ph.D., The Heritage Foundation, March 26, 2001, http://www.heritage.org/research/family/BG1421.cfm.

CHAPTER 5

1. "A Nation of Givers," Arthur C. Brooks, The American, March/April 2008 Issue, http://www.american.com/archive/2008/march-april-magazine-content

2. "Enron Scandal," Wikipedia, 8/11/2008, http://en.wikipedia.org/w/index.php?title=Enron_scandal&printable=yes

3. "Ex-Enron workers: 'Give 'em 50 years'," CNN Money, Steve Hargreaves, January 30, 2006, http://cnnmoney.com.

4. "Drug Lobby Second to None," Public Integrity, M. Asif Ismail, July 7, 2005, http://projects.publicintegrity.org/rx/report.aspx?aid=723.

5. Ibid.

6. "The Truth About Drug Companies," interview with Marcia Angell by Peter Meredith, September 7, 2004, http://MotherJones.com

7. "Report links high drug prices to marketing costs, executive payouts and profits," Families USA Report, familiesusa.org, year 2000 report, http://www.twnside.org.sg/title/twr131n.htm.

8. "Planting Seeds of Disaster," National Review Online, Stanley Kurtz, October 07, 2008, http://nationalreview.com

9. "Blame Fannie Mae and Congress For the Credit Mess," Charles W. Calomiris and Peter J. Wallison, The Wall Street Journal, September 23, 2008, http://online.wsj.com/article/SB122212948811465427.html.

10. "Planting Seeds of Disaster," National Review Online, Stanley Kurtz, October 07, 2008, http://nationalreview.com.

11. "Examples of Earmarks," grassfire.org, http://www.grassfire.org/96/resource.htm.

CHAPTER 6

1. "Less than 10 percent Believe Abortion should be Legal, Unfettered," One News Now, Charlie Butts, January 06, 2009, http://www.onenewsnow.com/Printer.aspx?id=371978.

2. "Parents Decision in Minor's Abortions Decisions," House Research Organization, Texas House of Representatives, April 30, 1999, http://www.hro.house.state.tx.us/focus/abortion.pdf

3. "Abortion in the United States: Statistics and Trends," National Right to Life, 2005, http://www.nrlc.org/ABORTION/facts/abortionstats.html

4. "Pregnancy Tips: Fetal Development during the First Trimester," Essortment, Lisa Vella, 2002, http://www.essortment.com/lifestyle/pregnancytipsn_sgdl.htm.

5. "Abortion Methods, Surgical Abortions," Life Site News, http://www.lifesitenews.com/abortiontypes/

6. "Abortion — Some Medical Facts," National Right to Life, http://www.nrlc.org/abortion/ASMF/asmf.html.

7. "U.S. Supreme Court Ruling Upholding Partial-Birth Abortion Ban Act," National Right to Life, 4/18/2007, http://www.nrlc.org/press_release_new/Release041807.html

8. "The Darwinian Basis for Eugenics," Anne Barbeau Gardiner, New Oxford Review, September 2008, http://www.newoxfordreview.org/reviews.jsp?did=0908-gardiner.

9.   Ibid.

10. "Margaret Sanger and Planned Parenthood: The Eugenics Connection," Angela Franks, National Right to Life, 2004, http://www.nrlc.org/news/2004/NRL07/margaret_sanger_and_planned_pare.htm.

11. Ibid.

12. "Abortion: Some Medial Facts — Psychological Consequences," National Right to Life, http://www.nrlc.org/abortion/ASMF/asmf4.html.

CHAPTER 7

1.   "Doc Knows Best," National Review, Jan. 6, 2003, http://www.nationalreview.com/comment/comment-smith010603.asp.

2.   "Tropical Rainforests are Regrowing. Now What?" Jan. 12, 2009, Deborah Zabarenko, Reuters, Http://reuters.com/article/environmentalNews/idUSTRE50B5CY20090112

3.   "Carbon Footprint," Wikipedia, 2/15/2009, http://en.wikipedia.org/wikicarbon footprint.

4.   "The Nine Lives of Population Control," Leadership U, Taken from First Things 38 (December 1993), Midge Decter, Pages 17-23, http://www.leaderu.com/ftissues/ft9312/articles/decter.html

5.   "Two Children Should be Limit, Says Green Guru," Sarah-Kate Templeton, Times Online, Feb.1, 2009, http://women.timesonline.co.uk/tol/life_and_style/women/families/

CHAPTER 8

1.   William Dannemeyer, *Shadow in the Land: Homosexuality in America* (San Francisco: Ignatius Press, 1989).

2.   Ibid., 120

3.   Ibid.

4.   Ibid., 121

5. Information gleaned from Anita's books, *The Anita Bryant Story* (1977), and *At Any Cost* (1978), and from Helen Kooiman Hosier's book *100 Christian Women Who Changed the 20ᵗʰ Century* (2000), all three books published by Baker/Revell.

6. Information gleaned from Dannemeyer's book, chapter entitled "The New Sex Education: Homosexuality."

7. Christian Clergy Rally on Opposite Sides of Gay Marriage Debate, http://www.christianpost.com/6/8/09.

8. Ibid.

CHAPTER 9

1. C. S. Lewis, *God in the Dock* (Grand Rapids, MI., William B. Eerdmans Publishing Co., 1970) 292.

2. Charles Colson, *Against the Night, Living in the New Dark Ages* (Ann Arbor, MI., Servant Publications, 1989), 10, 11.

3. David Aikman, *Great Souls: Six Who Changed the Century* (Nashville, TN., Word Publishing, 1998), 248.

4. Bill O'Reilly, *Culture Warrior* (New York: Broadway Books, 2006), 15.

5. Ibid., 20.

6. "The 12 Days of Michael," The Culture and Media Institute, a division of the Media Research Center, http://mail.google.com/mail/?ui=2&view=bsp&ver=1qygpcgurkovy

7. This material compiled from the *Life Application Study Bible, the New International Version* (Wheaton, Ill.: Tyndale Publishing House, Inc., 1988, 1989, 1990, 1991), Eph. 6:10-17.

8. Mark Galli, "Is the Gay Marriage Debate Over?" *Christianity Today,* July 2009, 33.

CHAPTER 10

1. Charles Colson, 107.

2.   Ibid., 163.

3.   A. W. Tozer, *The Knowledge of the Holy* (New York: Harper & Brothers, 1961). 47.

4.   Colson, 165-166.

5.   Ibid., 23, 24.

6.   http//mail.google.com/mail/?ui=2&view=bsp&ver=1qygpegurkovy

7.   Ibid.

8.   Ibid.

9.   Ibid.

10. Ibid.

11. Brad O'Leary, *The Audacity of Deceit* (Los Angeles, CA., WND Books, 2008), 101.

12. Ibid.

13. http//mail.google.com/mail/?ui=2&view=bsp&ver=1qygpegurkovy

14. Ibid.

15. Ibid.

16. Ibid.

17. Ibid.

18. Ibid.

19. Ibid.

20. canadafreepress.com/index.php/article/12652

21. Mark R. Levin, *Liberty and Tyrann: A Conservative Manifesto* (New York: Threshold Editions. A Division of Simon & Schuster, Inc., 2009)

22. Ibid.

CHAPTER 12

1.   C. S. Lewis, *Mere Christianity* (New York: MacMillan Publishing Co., Inc., 1943, 1945, 1952), 120.

2.   Ibid.,

3.   Tom Minnery, *Why You Can't Stay Silent: A Biblical Mandate to Shape Our Culture* (Wheaton, Ill.: Tyndale House Publishers, Inc., 2001), 25.

OTHER TITLES AVAILABLE BY GARY FRAZIER

Signs of the Coming of Christ

200 pages of exciting teaching concerning what the Bible says about specific indicators of the end times.

What Really Happens When Jesus Returns

A fictional novel that follows a family through a series of end time events.

It Could Happen Tomorrow, Future Events that will Change the World!

(Available as an audio book as well as print)

These items are available online at the following web sites:

www.DiscoveryMinistries.com

www.Amazon.com

LaVergne, TN USA
21 October 2009
161569LV00001BH/2/P